IRONS

IN THE

FIRE

.

by John McPhee

IRONS

IN THE

FIRE

JOHN

McPHEE

Farrar, Straus and Giroux

NEW YORK

Farrar, Straus and Giroux
18 West 18th Street, New York 10011

Copyright © 1997 by John McPhee

Printed in the United States of America
Published in 1997 by Farrar, Straus and Giroux
First paperback edition, 1998

The contents of this book originally appeared in The New Yorker.

The Library of Congress has cataloged the hardcover edition as follows:
McPhee, John A.
   Irons in the fire / John McPhee.— 1st ed.
      p. cm.
   ISBN-13: 978-0-374-17726-3
   ISBN-10: 0-374-17726-0 (alk. paper)
   I. Title.

AC8 .M417 1997
081—dc20

                                                    96-32358

Paperback ISBN-13: 978-0-374-52545-3
Paperback ISBN-10: 0-374-52545-5

www.fsgbooks.com

22 24 26 28 30 29 27 25 23 21

LAURA

CONTENTS

IRONS

IN THE

FIRE

.

In Princeton, New Jersey, where I live, I was having lunch not long ago with a friend just home from Nevada. He prospects there for precious metals, in the isolation country in the eastern part of the state, hundreds of miles from Reno and about as far from Las Vegas. Between the Horse Range and the Pancake Range, beside a crossroads café in Nye County, he had seen a bright-white vehicle with three antennas and an overhead bank of red and blue lights. On its side was the Great Seal of the State of Nevada, in the center of a gold seven-point star. It appeared to be the magnified badge of a sheriff, he said, but where he expected to see the words SHERIFF or STATE POLICE on the door, the words were not there. Instead, bold gold letters said, NEVADA BRAND INSPECTOR.

The prospector sipped the last of his coffee and, with some of his gold, got ready to pay the check. "Think what those words imply," he said.

I said, "What do they imply to you?"

"That these are the nineteen-nineties, and not the eighteen-nineties, but cattle rustling is alive and well in

Nevada," he said. "I thought of you when I saw those words on the door; I thought of what you might learn if, from basin to range, you could ride around that country with the brand inspector."

I got up, said goodbye to him, and departed for Nevada.

The brand inspector's white vehicle is known to him and his family as the state pickup. One antenna is for mountaintop repeaters, another for the highway patrol, the third for district car-to-car radio. The glove compartment is packed with ammunition—for the .38 special, for the Smith & Wesson .357 magnum revolver, for the High Standard sawed-off shotgun. In a box beside the driver are pads of brand-inspection certificates, piles of miscellaneous documents, and the state government's gold-stamped, cloth-bound, handsomely designed "Nevada Livestock Brand Book," which describes and sketches thirty-seven hundred and forty-three brands. He doesn't seem to need it. If you crack it open and ask him to describe the brand of, say, Bertrand Paris, he says, right back, "Reverse B Hanging P Right Ribs."

It's a busy brand that might tend to blotch. He prefers simplicity, as in the Rocking Arrow of Bertrand's grandson David.

The brand inspector's name is Chris Collis. He is forty, and of middle height and limber build. He is wearing a white cowboy hat, dark glasses, a plaid short-sleeved shirt, Levi's, a belt buckle made from the horn of a ram, and cowboy boots with two-inch heels. "It's a way of life," he is saying. "It's not an eight-to-five job." We are up in the Schell Creek Range, at nine thousand feet, in a forest of mountain mahogany. Aspens are already orange in the higher draws, chokecherry bushes red. The mountain mahogany is still green. The road is just a double track, and rocky, and he takes it very slowly. Coming out of the trees onto a bone-dry slope of sage and grassland, we look twenty-five miles over Spring Valley to the Snake Range. Grasshoppers are clicking, snapping. We pass a cow and a calf, another cow and her calf. Black Angus. "Feed stays longer in the mountains," he says. "Grass doesn't burn as much."

"What do they drink?"

"There are seeps among the aspens."

Wandering around on my own a couple of days ago, I crossed a cattle guard at ten thousand feet.

"Cattle start drifting off the mountain at this time of year," he goes on. "They know where they're going when it gets cool—if they were born here."

"Back east" is where the calves are going—to weight-making pastures and feedlots—but Chris means that cattle in the mountains at the end of summer will move in the direction of the valley ranches to which they belong, will sort themselves out with a homing instinct. They are rounded up as well, "gathered off the range," and then the calves are shipped. "This country here is cow/calf country. People don't put up enough feed for calves, so they sell them before winter." Every shipment must be certified in person by the district brand inspector, or by a deputy. Chris's district is, for the most part, White Pine, Nye, and Lincoln Counties, and covers an area about the size of New York

State. When Chris says that cattle are headed "back east," he usually means Colorado, or something close to Colorado. As it happens, he has never been farther east than that.

A calf is worth about a dollar a pound. "Every one of those calves is like a three-hundred-dollar bill sitting there," he says as—slowly descending—we pass more cow/calf pairs. Chris has found "strays" in southern Nye County that belong in Elko County. In other words, they strayed two hundred miles. "I think they had some help," he says gently. "Mistakes do happen." In White Pine County he has found "strays" from Roosevelt, Utah—two hundred and fifty miles measured with a string.

Stare as I will at the cattle, I have to ask him what the brands are. I'm not just suggesting that the brands are un-familiar. I'm saying that I can't even see them. Of course, I may be looking at the wrong side. Or I may be studying the shoulder when the brand is on the hip. But by and large I see only a few disjunct lines, not whole letters and whole numbers and geometric forms. I could not tell a Lazy S from a Rolling M if my life depended on it, or a Running F from a Lazy Walking A.

I see instead what appear to be old foundations under sod. "It's getting a little cooler now," he says tactfully. "They're beginning to hair up."

With the smallest touch of frustration, I ask him, "Do *you* see the brand on that one?"

"Yes."

His characteristic "Yes" is firm but slow. It has a lazy, lingering Y.

"What is the brand?"

"H Bar," he says. "Real low behind the shoulder. See it?"

"No."

Brands are like fish in a river—visible to the accomplished eye. As a matter of fact, I'm no good at seeing fish, either. Fly rod in hand, I have stood in paralytic outrage while someone shouted, "There! Right there! Don't you see them? Here they come! They're right beside you!" If these Angus cattle had my middle name on them, I wouldn't know it.

Brands will show best in raking light. "Sunshine is the brand inspector's best friend, and sometimes a shadow," Chris remarks.

Shirley Robison, his predecessor, now retired, has told me, "You can run cattle through just almost as fast as they can go, if you got the sun with you, you know, and if you're an experienced brand inspector. A lot of people can't see irons." It helps to be a tracker. Both Shirley and Chris can look at desiccated ground and note that a light sprinkling of rain fell on it for a few minutes two days before. "How would you know if you weren't raised to know that?" Shirley said. If you can learn to see a vanished rain shower, you can learn to see brands.

"My job is to make sure that neighbors don't ship other neighbors' cattle," Chris is saying. "But, if all a rancher does is put his iron on his neighbor's slick calf, intent is hard to prove. He'll just say it was a mistake." After a time, he adds, "I shouldn't know anybody's cattle better than they know their own. If you've got a cow that doesn't belong to you, it sticks out like a sore thumb."

Especially if it's slick—unbranded. A young unmarked animal is also known as an oreana, a maverick, a long-eared calf. If you find someone else's oreana mixed in with your cattle, you might be tempted to put your own iron on it—you might be tempted just to pocket that three-hundred-dollar bill. Slick bull calves and slick heifers aren't just everywhere, though, and a truly dedicated thief will need to alter existing brands. One does not have to be a Viennese forger to see that a Lazy E could become a Lazy Spiked E or a Lazy Right Up JM Combined.

Not that anyone with those brands would ever think of such a thing. I am merely offering some random possibilities as a result of a browse through the brand book. Routinely, the Livestock Identification Bureau, in Reno, sends Chris drawings of newly approved brands that are not yet in the book. His responsibility is to make sure that neighbors' brands are not similar. Once, for example, Reno sent him a Five Eight Combined.

An established brand on a ranch near the applicant's was Bar S Combined.

"It don't take too much imagination . . ." Chris says, his voice trailing off. After hearing from Chris, the bureau told the applicant to think up another brand.

In a general way, and without accusation, he has worried about how easily a Quartercircle V could turn into a Quartercircle M or a Quartercircle Flying V Bar.

And without too much running iron a Four Box could even turn into an AG Combined.

"If it was burned heavy, the open part of the G would look like an ordinary blotch."

The running iron is the rustler's traditional tool. It might be just an iron ring, tied to the saddle, or a conventional four-foot poker. You build a fire and use it to doctor a brand. The business end of most running irons is a short simple line. It becomes a red-hot stylus for metamorphic sketching. The business end of some running irons is as broad and flat as a playing card. You use that to blot out what you can't change. Be warned, though: there is pentimento in the hide—a history readable from within. Shirley Robison explained, "You take the critter and kill it, and have the hide tanned, and turn it over, and on the flesh side every iron shows just as plain as can be. Anyone can see where it's been altered or blotched."

In California some years ago, rustlers went off with three eighteen-wheelers full of cattle—a hundred-and-twenty-thousand-dollar robbery. Few people rustle cattle on that scale in Nevada, but to steal as much as one wet-nose calf is grand larceny. People with gooseneck trailers sometimes shoot cattle, speed-winch them into the trailers, and butcher them on the spot. The brand inspector is authorized to make arrests, but in country this size there's not much he can do to catch the butchers in the act. He has some help from the Secret Witness Program. A secret witness gets fifteen hundred dollars for information leading to the arrest and conviction of cattle rustlers.

There's a maxim in Nevada: "You don't ever eat your own beef." In other words, you steal it. You burn the hide. A variant is "You have to go to a neighbor's to taste your own beef." At a wedding, the host will thank his neighbors for supplying the beef.

A short Nevada chorus:

"You don't never eat your own beef."

"No one eats their own beef."

"Old Bob, he was a nice fellow to be around, but he liked to borrow the other guy's cow and eat his meat instead of his own."

The road follows a dry creek bed down toward the valley. The cattle we pass have split left ears and bell wattles—"marking" cuts, made during branding. They belong to a family named Eldridge, whose deeded land and range allotments include the mountains and the valley. With any change of ownership, cattle acquire an additional brand, and in the course of being sold by one rancher to another or to brokers who hold them on feedlots they come to look like living brand books, like vans covered with stickers.

"There are cattle that pack six irons."

If cattle run on a reservation, they have to carry the tribal iron with all the others—for example, the Duckwater Shoshone's Lazy Left YS Connected.

Not all brands are letters or numbers. You will see a range cow branded with a ladder, a leaf, a mitten, a mountain, a Boeing, a bow tie, or a fissioning bomb. In Minden, Nevada, the Hellwinkels' brand is COD. In Austin, Nevada, the Saraleguis' brand is COW.

As a calling, brand inspection derives from the gunfighters who were hired by the old cattlemen to protect their stock; and the detectives who were employed by livestock associations after the associations were formed, in the nineteenth century; and even the rustlers who were hired to prevent rustling. There is a little of all that in brand inspecting to this day. For the most part, the brand inspector is like a teacher taking frequent attendance in school. Much more is prevented than punished. If cattle are moved out of district or out of state, he is on hand to see each animal before it goes—even if ranchers are just trucking their own cattle between summer range and winter range, as many do. If cattle are changing ownership, the brand inspector certifies the change. When they are on their way to a sales yard, a feedlot, or a slaughterhouse, he is on hand to see them off. Otherwise, he rides around calling on people, or just punctuating the mountains and valleys with the white vehicle—making himself visible to as great an extent as possible. Where he is most visible, there is not much theft. There is not much theft within a hundred miles of his home, in Ely. He has thirteen part-time deputies. The Livestock Identification Bureau pays for itself. If the brand inspector inspects ten head, he collects six dollars; a thousand head, six hundred dollars. At all times of year, ranchers know, and are reassured to know, that he knows whose cattle are where, when they are moving, and when they should be moving. If he needs to, he will travel five hundred miles in one day to inspect them, getting up at 3 A.M. to be at a corral at daylight. There's only one auction yard in the state of Nevada. He goes to cattle gathered off the range.

Flouting the brand inspector is only a misdemeanor

unless it hides a larger crime. When uninspected cattle were shipped to California one time and Chris learned of it, he drove five hundred miles, to Bakersfield, just to make sure that a major heist had not been pulled. In a feedlot there, he found a hundred Nevada cattle eating culled carrots but only a single cow that the shipper did not own. One night in Diamond Valley when Shirley Robison was brand inspector, people on horseback rounded up about a hundred cattle and put them in a remote corral, and then loaded them into two trucks, undetected. Shirley felt he had reason to believe that the trucks went to Gonzales, California—to the feedlot known as Fat City, where pens held a hundred thousand cattle. Gonzales was even farther than Bakersfield. Shirley went there and, in a steady rainstorm, waded from pen to pen up to his knees in wet manure. The rustled cattle weren't there.

Chris once went to Hyrum, Utah—more than three hundred miles—in pursuit of a single animal, a heifer with Frankie Delmue's V Bar V Connected.

$$\bigvee\bigvee$$

He found her.

About one animal in twenty that he inspects is a horse. He uses the overhead blue and red lights when he stops trucks to ask to see certificates of inspection. Like many law-enforcement officers, he has had to put in a great many hours in court. "Defendants, they're never on trial," he says. "You're damned near naked up there on the witness stand."

Down at roughly sixty-five hundred feet, we move out onto a low alluvial fan and into Spring Valley. Far to our left, its flat horizon is flanked with mountains. Directly across the basin are mountains touching twelve thousand feet. Far to our right is a flat horizon flanked with mountains. This immense silent linear basin has a few clustered trees in it, tens of miles apart. The trees are exotic, introduced. Where you see a tree, there is something human underneath: the locus of the isolated lights you see in the basin at night. We come to an asphalt road—another pickup, headed south. We stop, get out. The other pickup stops, the driver joins us, and we talk there in the road, indefinitely. Chris introduces him as Gordon Eldridge. He is a rancher, and he runs his cattle on something like two hundred and fifty thousand acres. "It's as much as you can see," he says, in answer to a question and with an absence of grandeur or grandiosity. A typical ranch in these valleys will have as little as a hundred and sixty or as much as eight thousand acres of deeded, patented land, and the rest in allotments on federal range. Gordon Eldridge, cordially answering more questions, tells me that he has about three hundred and thirty cow/calf pairs in the Snake Range and four hundred in the Schell Creeks. He'll have them all in the valley for the winter. Unlike many others, he has springs and meadows and plenty of hay, and can afford to keep them on.

He wears a red visored cap, a blue canvas shirt, Levi's, and boots with wide low heels. He has been working nonstop, and his clothes are soiled from hat to shoes. One could say that he looks a great deal more like a mechanic than like a cowboy, except that a clear majority of cowboys here resemble mechanics. He is burly, and handsome in a large way: large lips, a thick face, alert eyes. He is about fifty and has an artificial leg. A horse fell on him in the mountains. He spent the night there freezing. He could easily have died.

His children's high school is sixty miles away.

Is there a problem about thievery in this valley?

"Oh, yes," he says. "If a cow comes up short a calf,

there are several possibilities: a mountain lion got it, or it died some other way, or people got it. You see crows flying. A magpie. One year, we were short ten calves. We find most of the ones that die. I know when people are operating, coming through the country. This isn't my first rodeo."

He looked around for a while, called attention to a dead fox in the road, and then said, "The brand inspectors just keep the people straight. Without them, people would be hauling cattle back and forth and we wouldn't know what they're doing. If you didn't have them, everybody—lots of people—would be stealing cattle for a living. They keep people honest, just knowing they're in the country. We've always thought it was good for the country."

Other ranchers, in other valleys, amplify the sentiment. For example, Norman Sharp, in Railroad Valley: "What if *what*? No brand inspector? There'd be a lot of dead bodies."

Chet Johnson, in White River Valley: "It'd be a disaster. Oh, shit, it'd just be a free-for-all. Cattle rustling is an occupational hazard. I'm surrounded with thieves."

I was spending a day with Shirley Robison, the retired brand inspector, when, in the following manner, I met Chet Johnson. In my rented Utah blue Chevy, Shirley and I were humming south on a paved road in White River Valley, under the Egan Range. A G.M.C. pickup, coming north and also moving rapidly, shot past us. Shirley said, "That's Chet Johnson. Turn around and turn on your lights." I slowed, braked, and spun around. By now, the pickup was about half a mile up the road. I switched on the lights. Immediately, the pickup pulled over. The driver, seeing a car in his valley, had been watching it. "That's ranch country!" Shirley said. "That's ranch country. You see, that's the way things work here." By the time we had closed the distance and stopped behind the pickup, Johnson was leaning his back against it, waiting. He was a tall, compelling man wearing a copper bracelet, black boots, Levi's, a small and conventional belt buckle, a brown canvas shirt, and a white cowboy hat. A longhorn Brahma bull had once hit a horse right out from under him and killed the horse. When he used the word "surrounded"—as in "surrounded with thieves"—the word had less immediacy than it would have in most contexts. His place ran about sixty miles this way and forty miles that. He said it was "damned hard to patrol." He said, "People just drive your cows on their place and brand 'em, even if they're branded already. There's not a hell of a lot you can do. Brand inspectors keep it down. Some people need a lot of watchin', even with a good brand inspector. Without the brand inspector, we'd have to go back to the eighteen-hundreds and start hangin' 'em. In fact, it's so hard to prosecute 'em we need to go back to that hangin'."

Shirley Robison, who had seen his share of mountain lions, coyotes, and defense lawyers, said, "That hangin'—we should go back to that. String 'em to the first tree."

Leaning against the pickup, I was looking due west, fifteen miles across the valley. There was no first tree.

In the great treeless valleys, pickups, with their wakes of dust, stand out like speedboats. "When you have five cows get away and come home with fresh brands on them, you have no idea how many went to Colorado," Johnson said. "There's somebody pecking at them all the time, and if you see a dust out there you go and check it out. Something's going on all the time."

Now Gordon Eldridge, in Spring Valley, reaches into a shirt pocket and removes a small ledger containing the license numbers and the makes of unknown vehicles that he has seen in the valley since who knows when. In these two hundred and fifty thousand acres, vehicles are so infrequent that he has no difficulty being thorough. "We can't watch our cattle, so we watch the people," he says. "We track the people. My dad taught me to track a coyote across the highway; it don't leave much print." He tracks lions, too. "A lion can tear a horse's shoulder off. Lions kill a lot of mustangs. They kill those big old four-point bucks. They wait in the narrows of the canyons. Coyotes kill both calves and sheep. We were lambing sheep over there in those hills one time, and coyotes were killing lambs every night. One coyote was carrying the lambs seventeen miles to its den. My dad tracked 'im. He found all kinds of legs there. They don't eat the legs. Dad tracked 'im seventeen miles on horseback." Gordon returns the book to his pocket, remarking that the motives and motions of people are a good deal less difficult to follow than the tracks of lions and coyotes. "There was a gold swindler in the valley, looking for investors, and he told us that he got gold in a cave in the Snake Range. People can't come out here and fool us. We're crusty old buggers."

Twenty-five miles down the valley, in late slanting light, Chris turns in at Lonne Gubler's Cleveland Ranch, where Cleve Creek comes out of the mountains and productively waters the basin. There are, in addition, so many springs and so much meadow that cattle can remain here eleven months a year. Over the wide valley they look like chocolate bugs. A while ago, the brand inspector caught Gubler transporting uninspected calves and gave him a citation that resulted in a hundred-and-fifty-dollar fine. This in no way chills the brand inspector's welcome as he greets ranch hands, opens and closes gates, and bumps on out into the middle of the basin to put us among a thousand calves and cows. He is inspecting nothing. He is just visiting the cattle. Leaving the pickup, he walks about a hundred yards, and they skittishly run away from him, alert and fearful, wise to his kind. They could not care less that he's a brand inspector, but from animals that look like him almost all of them have felt the burn of brands.

They run in groups. They run alone. They run away. But then Chris lies down on his back, and, taking his cue, I sit on the ground near him. He raises one leg in the air. All the cattle turn their heads and stop in their tracks. They watch. They are not threatened. A sudden switch from fear to curiosity has taken place in their cavernous bicameral minds. The brand inspector is now lying on his side, propped on one elbow, maintaining the leg semaphore. Cattle move some steps toward him. More join in. More. Dozens more. A hundred. They have formed a great semicircle with him as gnomon. You can read the hour in the shadow of his leg: 5 P.M. Angus, Angus-Hereford crosses, Brangus, Charolais, Simbrah—about once a minute, they take another step forward, virtually in unison. The semicircle curls around until it is nearly a full circle of yearling heifers, flank to flank and head by head, benignly staring. "It takes two years to get a calf out of them," Chris remarks in a soft voice.

"How long will they last?"

"Until their teeth break. You'll see their teeth breaking pretty good at least by ten. Few cows are over twelve here."

He reels in his foot and assumes a cross-legged sitting position. Some very big cottonwoods stand nearby. Wheeler Peak, twenty miles away, looms above this scene with the imminence of the trees. We are almost exactly a mile above sea level, and Wheeler Peak is a mile and a half higher than we are. Wheeler Peak and numerous summits elsewhere in this state are not much lower than the highest mountains of Colorado and California—hardly the picture that outlanders see when they imagine Nevada.

I remark, "These animals look well fed, healthy, and expensive."

He says, "Fat is the prettiest color in the cattle business."

Out in the flats, coyotes are wailing like theft alarms.

The cattle, silent, show no interest in the sound of coyotes. All take another step forward. The circle tightens. And still another step. It closes. In their curiosity, they have built around two human beings a beef corral. They occlude the falling sun and study us through twilight. As my gaze slowly moves among these candid faces, these guileless open nonjudgmental faces—from one frank stare to the next—I see behind them future shoes. These are the faces of big spotted owls, of snail darters and three-spined sticklebacks. These are, to a fare-thee-well, endangered specimens. In their soft, tanned appearance you can see the belts and briefcases. There is chewing gum in a cow, soft cartilage for plastic surgery, floor waxes, glues, piano keys. There are detergents, deodorants, crayons, paint, shaving cream, shoe cream, pocket combs, textiles, antifreeze, film, blood plasma, bone marrow, insulin, wallpaper, linoleum, cellophane, and Sheetrock.

The sun is behind the mountains. We stand up to leave. They scatter like fish.

Some days later, and soon after school, Chris stops off at home to pick up his wife, his children, and his horses and take them to do branding at a ranch in Duck Creek Valley. The horses are Luke and Fuzzhead, sorrel geldings. They are in a pasture of about four acres beside the house and barn, on the outskirts of Ely. Neither Luke nor Fuzzhead wants anything to do with the ranch in Duck Creek Valley. They elude capture. From fence to fence they gallop, manes streaming. As Chris runs after them, they stay out of the corners. They know what they're doing. They are expressing themselves with regard to the work ethic. Christopher Collis, aged ten, crewcut, removes his spurs, hands them to his mother, and runs into the pasture to assist his father. The two of them close in on the horses. The horses slip away, and run a hundred yards. A cool wind is blowing through this scene with valley and mountains behind it. Steptoe Valley. Camel Peak, of the Duck Creek Range. A new G.M.C. pickup and gooseneck trailer stand by, empty. The trailer's neck arches into the back of the pickup and attaches to the floor of the bed. There's a basketball hoop, exactly ten feet high. A dish antenna. Two bleating lambs. Karen Collis, with the spurs in her hand, looks patient. Her father is Gracian Uhalde, who trails five thousand sheep a hundred miles, between Steptoe Valley and Garden Valley, between summer range and winter range, twice a year. Her grandfather was a Basque from the French Pyrenees. Five feet tall and trim as a wand, she keeps her hair short and has small diamond studs in her ears. The new, metal barn has four stalls and a large space containing a Buick, a Chevy pickup, and a Cadillac El Dorado, which have a combined age of fifty-nine years. The house, one story, has a wide carport running all the way down one long side. It shelters firewood. Inside, there's a stone bearing wall and a big stove and a framed sampler: "Ewe's Welcome." Inside also are Gerry, aged nine, and Eleni, six. When their mother calls, they come tumbling out, Eleni in pink leggings, Gerry in a cap that says "ROPER." The horses have been bought off with a bucket of grain, time to go.

Twelve miles up Steptoe Valley is McGill, where Chris was born—a Kennecott company town. The copper smelter is gone now, completely disassembled. His family rig—an extended-cab pickup and horse trailer—rolls up Fourth Street, the principal thoroughfare. On the uphill side of Fourth, the uniform houses are somewhat larger than the houses on the ground that dips toward the center of the valley. The house he grew up in was on the lower side, in a neighborhood known as Greek Town, which was near Austrian Town, with a buffer of Mexicans between. "Then all the white people lived above Fourth Street," he remarks, "white" apparently meaning comparatively well-to-do. His late father worked in the accounting office. Chris seems to have nothing but nostalgia for the beneficial Kennecott. He went to high school in Ely and college in Reno, where he studied animal science at the University of Nevada. He was teaching at the university and working toward a master's degree when, on Shirley Robison's retirement, he came home to be the brand inspector.

North of McGill, Steptoe Valley broadens, and, between its lateral ranges, goes so far beyond sight that we seem to be heading for open sea. Before long, though, we take a right, and climb over the Duck Creeks to a narrow mountain valley above seven thousand feet. This is where Chris has sixty-seven head of cattle, in rented pasture, on a ranch still owned by Kennecott. He took out a bank loan earlier in the year and bought the cattle, for the purpose of producing calves and gradually accumulating enough money to educate his children. The children are here to work, too, and in that sense will be self-educated. Ten-year-old Christopher, in his camouflage cap and Tonopah Test Range T-shirt, buckles on his spurs, mounts Fuzzhead, a big horse, and rides off to the north. His father—who calls him "pard" and "pardner"—follows on Luke. Watching them with mild interest is a six-point elk. The elk moves on. Christopher and his father round up forty-four head while his mother walks the pasture as a third party in the shaping of motion. Gerry waits. I wait. Six-year-old Eleni, in her pink leggings and matching top, waits. She sits on the high rail of a small circular corral. There is a large adjacent holding corral—a rectangular pen—and her brother, father, and mother are attempting to influence the cattle in its direction.

Cattle are indeed like fish in the way they school and spook. To move them from place to place is to use to advantage their reliable desire to get away from human beings, which is derived from instinct, enhanced by conditioned response, and informed by common sense. A bit of stick, a little shout, they hurry by. They are also clever at slipping away, like basketball players: they move well to the left and the right; they reverse-pivot; they go back door. Eleni, on the corral fence, is playing electronic one-on-one basketball on a small machine in her hand: Michael Jordan versus Larry Bird. At White Pine County High School, her father played basketball, in the backcourt. When White Pine played Rancho High in North Las Vegas, two hundred and eighty-one miles away, he was matched up man-to-man with Lionel Hollins, who went on to play for Arizona State and then for the Portland Trail Blazers and the Philadelphia 76ers and other N.B.A. teams. When White Pine played Clark High School in Las Vegas, Chris was assigned to Willie Smith, who later played for the University of Missouri and for Portland and Cleveland in the N.B.A. At the University of Nevada, Chris went out for the rodeo team and became a varsity roper.

The forty-four cattle move to the holding corral as their other options are sequentially eliminated. Lacking romals (four-foot flexible rawhide whips), Chris and Christopher snap at the cattle with the ends of their coiled nylon ropes. The ropes are forty-five feet long and thirty-five feet long, and are made of braided nylon scarcely thicker than a quarter inch. ("You want a small fast rope.") Into the smaller, tight corral they drive the cow/calf pairs, until the space is jammed with cattle. Then, riding among them, the two swiftly cut out and drive out most of the cows, leaving in the small corral a huddle that is mainly calves. Karen closes the gate. Christopher "throws a loop to catch a critter." He misses. His dad throws a loop to catch a critter. He misses. Christopher has been on horseback for seven years and has been working much of that time. His siblings, too, have been in the saddle from the age of three. Christopher, serious and competent, who rounds up wild horses on the open range, and rounds up cattle and brings them to corrals, and throws his loops, and dallies his rope, and helps to brand, and does all the rest of it, is nevertheless ten years old, a child still, a fifth grader, and at home he plays with toys. They are ranch toys—little loading chutes, and miniature trucks, and polyethylene corrals, and plastic calves—and he finds no end of absorption in them, and will play with them hour after hour, until it's time for bed, or time for homework, or time to go off to some real valley, mount a real horse, and do the real thing. He freelances. At a ranch a hundred miles from Ely, he rode roundup for the Fallinis this year. Gratefully, they gave him those two lambs he has at home, and a Hereford calf. Gerry and Eleni are not much interested in ranch toys.

In the tight corral with the bunched calves, Chris and Christopher are throwing traps so fast that they become in my scribbled notes C-1 and C-2:

C-2, roping, misses. C-1, roping, misses. C-2 gets bull calf in one leg, loses him, drops rope. C-1 misses. Mom coils C-2's rope. C-1 ropes two legs, but loses him or her. C-1 ropes a calf, yells to wife, "Get on him!" Before Karen can get on him, the calf gets away. C-1 misses again. C-2 misses. C-1 ropes a calf by both hind legs. Mom is on her. Calf bawling. Eleni crying. Mom sits on head. Charolais heifer, stretched out. Eyes bulging. C-1 dismounts. Gerry, 9, gets on dad's horse, holds rope taut to calf. C-1 gets vaccination gun, injects calf for blackleg, malignant edema, overeating disease, and red water. Mom is kneeling on calf, holding its leg. Mom is a surgical nurse. She works in the O.R. at William Bee Ririe Hospital, Ely.

Chris is apologetic: "We mainly do this in the spring. We're kind of rusty." Most calves are branded just after they are gathered off the winter range. These slicks are the latecomers, the overlooked, the whatever. When you're heeling, or roping, you make a loop through the honda at the end of the rope, and swing it, and throw it. The thrown loop is called a trap.

"When I threw my trap on that first calf, I should have had him."

The trap is thrown between the front and the rear legs, with the loop standing. The calf in that instant walks over the bottom of the loop, and you draw it up. You dally the rope—make turns around the saddle horn. You can lose your fingers. Chris has a rope-burn scar on his thumb from last June. The rope went almost to the bone. The horse, turning, keeps the rope taut and drags the calf to the fire. At the fire, the horse turns again to face the calf, backing up to keep the line taut. Quick-eyed Gerry with the "ROPER" hat, up on Luke the horse.

The Collises' fire is propane, in a small ovenlike shield, and it is hissing beneath the branding stamps on the ends of the irons. The shafts of the irons fan out like sticks from a campfire. People who still use wood to heat irons haul the cedar, the piñon, the juniper from the mountains. There are immobilizing calf tables now, and hydraulic squeeze chutes, wherein the calf becomes the filling of a steel-bar sandwich and is hydraulically rolled to the horizontal to be stencilled with a hot electric iron. Wood and propane tend not to supply uniform heat. "An electric iron gives you a consistent type of iron," Chris says. But in Nevada the predominant method is still to "rope 'em and drag 'em to the fire."

A stamp brand with scupper holes will tend to make a neat impression—like, for example, old John Ansolabehere's Lazy E Over P.

The scupper holes are a way to avoid making what Shirley Robison has called "a burnt gob on the side of a critter." When the brand, cherry red, goes on, the heat dissipates in the holes, but the holes fill in. "The better irons are simple irons," Chris says. "Some get awful fancy, but all they are is blotch. There's too much iron, too much heat." His and Karen's original brand tended to blotch. It was the Greek letter Psi.

Elegant as a chalice, it filled too often. So they registered a new and simpler brand.

"The brand is a cow's return address," Chris remarks. "That Quartercircle Standing Quartercircle can be put on by anyone. You don't want your brand to embarrass you."

While Gerry keeps the rope taut and his mom continues to kneel on the calf, his dad, on foot, takes an iron from the fire and causes a puff of smoke to rise from the calf's right hip. The two new moons appear. "That's how a fresh brand should look—buckskin color," Chris remarks, returning the iron to the fire. (A buckskin horse is a yellow horse.) Ever mindful not to touch the ground with the iron, he says, "Manure burns forever. You have to be careful." He opens a knife. The calf, which was bawling, is now staring wildly but is silent. Chris folds the right ear. Into the crease he cuts a semicircle, making a hole in the center of the ear. He moves the blade from the hole through the pink flesh to the point of the ear—a longitudinal slit—as if he were cutting fruit. In the tip of the other ear he makes a notch. These are the family's registered earmarks. Earmarking is restrained by a Nevada statute: "It shall be unlawful for any owner . . . to use an earmark which involves the removal of more than one-half of the ear . . . or which brings the ear to a point by removing both edges."

Christopher ropes two heifers—a Saler cross and then a Hereford. His mom holds them, and his dad brands them.

Dad sails his loop to the ground, and leaves it there for a long count, lying flat, as another Hereford heifer walks over it. He jerks the line upward and the loop closes around the hind legs. This is known as "fishing it on the calf." Mom falls on the calf's neck. The calf is bawling, branded.

Calf No. 5 is a Saler-cross bull calf. C-2 ropes him on right rear leg, drops rope. Mom picks up rope, returns it to C-2. Dad dismounts. Gerry mounts Luke. Rope comes off leg. Calf fights free. New No. 5 is full-blood Saler bull calf, roped on one hind leg, screaming. Dad lifts him, flips him, marks his ears. He slices off the tip of the scrotum as if he were scissoring the tip of a cigar. He squeezes into the light the pearl-gray glistening ellipsoid oysters. He does not cut the cords but works them with the blade—scraping, shaving, thinning until they part. The process greatly reduces loss of blood. The calf's eyeballs, having rotated backward, are two-thirds white. Mom stands attentive with an aerosol can of screwworm-fly spray. She passes it to Dad. The spray emerges royal blue, and coats the scrotal wound. Antiseptic and fly repellent, it keeps maggots from hatching there.

"Who's going to eat the oysters?" Christopher says.

Calf No. 6 is also a bull. These are not young calves, and they are hard to hold. They weigh at least three hundred pounds. At last, this one is stretched out, bawling, tongue protruding far, eyeballs largely white. From the bunched animals across the corral a cow emerges, boldly approaches the people and the prostrate calf, and smells it. Identification positive. He is hers. She goes on snuffling him but does not become aggressive. "Some cows would try to hook or butt you," Chris remarks. Six-year-old Eleni, down from the fence, has put away Bird and Jordan, and, nurselike, close to the procedure, is holding the vaccination gun and the antiseptic spray. "Get behind him," her father tells her, accepting the vaccine. He tries to hand her the oysters. She says firmly, "I don't want 'em." Soon Gerry is carrying a cup of oysters. Hereabouts, they appear on menus as entrées. "They are real rich, like sweetbreads," Chris says. "You've probably had mountain oysters before. You cook them in a Dutch oven. You brown them in oil and garlic, and bake them. They are also called fries."

The cow is carrying five brands, including the DB Combined of Donald Dee Eldridge, the JY Bar Connected of Jerry Millett, the Bar Over DM of Denny Manzonie, the Lazy Left YS Connected of the Duckwater Shoshone, and the Collises' Quartercircles.

A few more calves, and the evening's work is done. The sun is down. Eleni is now on Luke. Her pink sneakers do not reach the stirrups. She just sits up there, a small inverted Y, in her pink-and-purple-flowered outfit, looking very miniature and very competent. With Christopher, she means to get the cattle moving back to pasture. To get them out of the corral, he wants to drive them counterclockwise, but she kick-starts her horse and moves them clockwise. She directs the drive through the pens to pasture. It's just a matter of hang time.

"It takes nine months to make a calf and eight to get it to four hundred pounds, and in another five months you can almost double that weight," Chris says. "You sell pounds." In three locations, he has an aggregate of a hundred and twenty-one cow/calf pairs, and before long he will have two hundred. A cow will give him a calf a year. ("If I have a cow and she's not pregnant, she's not going to the winter range.") That should cover some tuitions. It should help the team.

There's a coyote watching as the Collises leave the high valley. A new moon has come into the sky, a standing sliver, right off their brand.

Will James was convicted of cattle rustling in White Pine County. He was Québécois, and his real name was Dufault. He was better at concealing his personal identity than that of the stolen cattle. Only twenty-two, he was still an amateur writer and artist but already a seasoned cowboy. The year was 1914. Near Johns Wash Well, east of the Fortification Range, he and another rider, drifting south, came upon thirty-one head and recognized from the brands that the cattle had drifted, too, and were far from their home range. Hiding in hills and moving at night, James and the partner drove them into Utah, but, since nothing much moves in this country unobserved, James spent the next year and a half polishing his artistic talent behind bars.

In a conversation with Shirley Robison, the brand inspector emeritus, I learned that rustlers are cattle as well as people—a terminological knot. "Angus–Hereford crosses are very popular—they're good rustlers," Shirley said.

I said, "They are good *what*?"

"Rustlers. They're good at finding feed and trailing back and forth between the water and the feed in these long distances out on these alluvial benches and stuff. They'll get out and rustle. Those Angus cows will go clear back up in the hills here and then come back down to water. There is cattle that are worthless. You've got to get rid of 'em. They won't go out. They'll stand and half starve to death, and won't rustle for food."

We were travelling south, over ruts that were not quite road, on the Forest Moon Ranch, in White River Valley. He was revisiting the scene of the last major crime of his tenure (he retired in 1979). In the seventies, Hot Creek was the name of the Forest Moon. Its owner, John Gurley, hired a new foreman, named Ross Rytting. As any good foreman would, Rytting at once busied himself getting familiar with the ranch terrain—every wash, draw, arroyo, dip, and depression in country where a hundred miles is as far as the eye can see. His eye, evidently, was arrested particularly by the scant remains of a nineteenth-century homestead.

Under cottonwoods and a dead apple, it was in a meander
bend of the Moon River—an expansively named little spring
creek—a mile and a half downvalley from the ranch buildings and fifteen feet lower in elevation: in other words, from
the point of view of the ranch, hidden from sight. The
homesteaders had lived in a half dugout, snuggled into a
small river terrace; and around the dugout, with flat rocks,
Rytting quickly built a stone corral. That, at any rate, was
Robison's reconstruction of events. He first saw the scene,
of course, after the fact—saw the tracks, the treads, the
manure, the corral, and a crude stone chute. A foreman
who rustles should think in small numbers—think six at a
time will never be missed. Six can bring as much as two
thousand dollars. Six fill a gooseneck and do not need a
large truck. A large truck coming into the valley at an odd
time would attract only a little less attention than would the
QE2 coming up the Moon River.

With the impressive new foreman in place, John and
Mrs. Gurley went off on vacation. Scarce had the dust settled
behind them when Rytting got into his pickup, drove down
to the old homestead with a horse trailer, loaded six calves
he had sequestered there, and headed for Utah. Heifers and
steers, they were six months old. They had not travelled ten
miles when someone in White River Valley saw the trailer,
saw that it had cattle in it, wondered what that was all about,
and telephoned the brand inspector to let him know. When
Shirley tells the story, he relishes the irony that the Gurleys
that evening had checked into Ely's Hotel Nevada—a sa-
loon with beds, dating from the nineteen-twenties, with ancient brands all over a wall—and "if Gurley had looked out
a window he could have seen his own calves going by in
his own trailer." Up the long spare valleys with their far-
spread lonely lights, Shirley tracked the cattle by telephone.
Not for him the posse chase. There was method, though,

in this relaxed approach to police work. Nevada is not a
plexus of roads. A vehicle in motion in Nevada is like a ship
on a set course. This one seemed to be going out of state,
and that is where Shirley hoped to track it. He talked with
a deputy brand inspector in Wendover (on the state line),
and his instructions were simple: "Let him go."

Shirley had developed a preference for federal courts.
"A little judge can be bought off," he will say. "A federal
court, the politicians can't get at it." Never mind that "the
U.S. Attorney wouldn't know a cow from a pig."

There was a regular livestock sale in Ogden. Ogden
was more than a hundred and fifty miles from Wendover,
but that was where the calves would be going. Shirley called
the brand inspector there. "I told him to put the biggest
padlock in Utah on those cattle, that they were stolen. And
then I called the F.B.I. in Salt Lake. The F.B.I. said, 'We'll
take over.' " Rytting, arraigned, was released on bail.

Three F.B.I. agents were assigned to the case—a ratio
approximating one pound of agent per two pounds of beef.
Shirley told me, "They confiscated the calves, loaded 'em
up, and then one agent drove the pickup and two agents
followed—one in front, one in back. They didn't want that
chain of evidence to be broke. Those calves were gone three
days. They never did get out of the trailer."

At Shirley's request, Chet Johnson, whose place abut-
ted Hot Creek Ranch, rode with some hands into Hot Creek
grazings to search out and round up tight-bagged cows.
Easily, they found the mothers, and took them to a Hot
Creek corral. The ranch structures under old cottonwoods
are neat in appearance, shaded, and cool. They stand below
a limestone butte capped with quartzite—freestanding in
the basin, like a floating vessel, sheer, eight hundred feet
high. Into this milieu came Shirley Robison with three F.B.I.
men and six calves. He had connected with them in Ely.

Shirley continues the story: "We undone those calves, and we put them in with the big-bag cows, and the agents had a movie camera, see, and we took movies of the whole thing: the calves matin' back up and suckin', you know. And a cow don't allow—a range cow, especially, don't allow—another calf around. We matched 'em all. We had 'em all suckin' within fifteen minutes. We made movies of each calf as it mothered up to its mother and started to suck."

Some time later, Shirley was the recipient of a threatening phone call from a man who did not identify himself, a man who had a voice like a tuba. He said, "You smart brand-inspector son of a bitch, you better pull off before you're in trouble."

Shirley said, "Who are you, Mister?"

The man said, "Look, you brand-inspector bastard. Pull your God-damned horns in before it's too late."

Shirley in his youth was a Golden Gloves boxer. One of six brothers, he grew up near the Sinks of Baker, in a basin so remote that his high school had two rooms, two teachers, and thirty students. He played basketball there, and the name of every player on the team was Robison. He always had his own boxing gloves, and wore out a pair a year. He learned to fight by fighting his brothers. Shirley—six feet, solid—has a trim trapezoidal mustache, a squarish face, and hair enough on either arm to cover anyone's head. Holding his telephone, he felt some of the hair move, and he said to the caller, "You cowardly dog! You come to my face and say that. Let me know who you are. You're a coward."

"It could have been anybody," Shirley says, telling the story.

Several months went by before the federal court in Reno heard the case of the Hot Creek cattle. When Ross Rytting took the stand, Shirley was looking at Rytting for the first time ever, and he lied like a tuba. But Shirley had what it took to put him away. "He got four years. Which isn't enough. They used to hang 'em, you know."

Shirley was not often able to chase down a rustler by telephone. He had to get up in the ranges and out in the basins—far from Ely, his home and base as brand inspector, far from much of anything—to gather his evidence and, when necessary, capture cattle-rustling women and men. Being far from Ely was, after all, his birthright geography. When his family said that something was "in town," they meant Ely. It was sixty miles away. "I bought my clothes by mail order from National Bellas Hess, Montgomery Ward, and Sears. I never went to Ely until I was a grown kid. You betcha. My granddad came into this country, alone, in 1873, when he was thirteen."

Shirley's most complicated case involved a woman and two men who were thought to be preying on the cattle of the brothers Sharp. The Sharps lived in Railroad Valley, in Nye County, a long distance from a telephone, and a much longer distance from the nearest railroad, there never having been one anywhere near Railroad Valley. The Sharps were "good boys," in Shirley's view. "Good old country boys. Very economical ranchers. Don't spend anything." One of the things they didn't spend was a great deal of time keeping track of their cattle—patrolling their ranchlands and range allotments, which were comparable in size to a modest sea. And so—over two or three years—the clandestine rustlers were able to take something on the order of twelve hundred head. "That's how they made their living. They just about had the Sharp brothers flat on their back."

When Shirley's help was finally sought, he was before long inconvenienced to discern that there seemed to be a couple of masterminds behind the rustling operation, for he thought that one of the masterminds was the head of what is now the Livestock Identification Bureau, in Reno, while the other was John Casey. "The worst two words you can say in the state of Nevada are John Casey," Shirley remarked one day while we were driving toward Baker with his wife, Marge. "You betcha. Those are the two nastiest words you can say to any rancher. John's still alive. They had him on TV, and made a special thing about thieves here, a while back, and he looked just like a rattlesnake, slippery as an eel."

Marge said, "He's not to be trusted."

Shirley was not overwhelmed by the fact that his boss might be implicated. You can't judge a crook by his cover. The first rustler that Shirley ever caught had been someone he grew up with. There is an intimacy in Nevada in inverse proportion to the great open space. You betcha, he was undeterred—just cramped somewhat—but he sent word up an ancillary grapevine to Governor Paul Laxalt, in Carson City, who sent a plane to fetch him (Nevada One) and flew in District Brand Inspector Arshal Lee, from Lincoln County, as well. Laxalt told them that they were now reporting to him and to "go and get the job done."

They narrowed their attention to a spring creek in the mountains at the nose of the Quinn Canyon Range. There was an abandoned ranch—the old Bardoli place—and the rustlers were believed to be there. Across the mountains to the east was Garden Valley, into which came a wash called Cherry Creek. Up Cherry Canyon, at a place called Adaven, they began their careful and stalking approach. (Adaven— its population long since zero—had been named by somebody who figured out what that spelled backward.) Above seven thousand feet, they stashed the state pickup behind Cherry Creek Summit, and proceeded on foot down the Ox

Spring Wash and nearly a mile past Burnt Canyon. They stopped where they could look down a west-facing slope half a mile to a small corral. The spring creek was there, and—two hundred yards from the corral—"a shacky frame house, little more than a cabin." They saw a watchful gaggle of domestic geese; they saw dogs. They waited. Day after day, they waited. They camped in Sawmill Canyon, on the far side of the crest of the range, and returned each morning, six miles, in the same manner. They could work only in daylight. They would have to see the brands. At last, a small truck appeared, carrying cattle, and followed by a pair of riders. Two men. The driver of the truck was a woman. They left the cattle in the corral and went to the house.

Shirley went down to read the brands. He walked, crawled, and slid the half mile. He used cedars and piñons for cover, completely conscious that he could be killed if discovered. Where he had to cross open ground, as he did most of the way, he lay on his back and inched downhill.

"If I tried to get on my hands and knees, there'd be too much of me exposed. I stayed as low as I could into the brush."

Nearing the corral, he managed not to arouse the dogs, and he skirted the pit-bull geese. But the rustlers also kept a flock of sentinel pigeons.

"And I got past the dogs and I got past the geese—they were away from me now, they were a hundred and fifty yards over here, but a dog can usually pick you up, you know, and so can a goose—but the damned pigeons spotted me, and they dive-bombed me. They'd come right down over me. And I figured they'd give me away. But I finally got in back of the corral and got out of sight, really, until things settled down and they flew on away."

Looking through the corral fence, he saw three long-eared calves, three Hereford cows, and two brands.

Both the Cross L Combined and the Quartercircle Lazy E were registered under the names of Norman and Gerald Sharp.

You can't read a brand on the far side of a cow, and the uncoöperative cows had just stood there presenting their unbranded sides.

"You have to wait for 'em to turn around. I would flip rocks in so I didn't make much movement, you know, so anyone would see me; I would flip rocks in so I could get 'em to turn around till I could read the brands, see?"

Creeping, sliding, hiding his way uphill, Shirley retreated.

Later, he and Arshal watched the rustlers take the cows away, leaving the calves. They took the cows to a field. Shirley and Arshal approached on foot, and hid near the field behind trees.

"Those guys . . . We were down so damned close. We got down onto 'em close enough to hear 'em fart."

They were hearing Barney Simpson and John Casey, Jr.

Casey and Simpson had a .22 pistol and used it on the brains of the cows. At the firecracker ping of the first shot, numerous pigs, appearing out of nowhere, came running.

"Bang—they'd shoot 'em in the head. And, when they banged, pigs of all sizes—from big old mature sows to little bitty pigs—come ascreamin' and asqueelin'. If there was one, there was sixty. They knew they were going to get fed. And we sit there and watched Barney Simpson and John Casey, Jr., and they used big knives and would slice on the shanks and the belly and open everything up so the pigs could get right in. The pigs ate it all but the paunch. I mean, we're that close enough to watch this. I mean, we're right against them, see? They didn't see us. We made damned sure they didn't. If they'd have known we were there, they'd have cut us up and fed us to the pigs. We'd have just been skulls out there, rolling around with the pigs. They were unkind people. They were giggling. They were proud of what they were doing. They were feedin' those pigs off'n the cows and stealin' the long-eared calves, see? And they were pretty slick at it, I'll tell you. But they have no godliness. They have no godliness."

Not far from this scene, a week or so before, Shirley had discovered a burning ghat for bones. "I mean, big stacks of burned bones, as deep as my arm. They were all sawed up." The rustlers were cutting the brands out of the cow-hides and burning the brands as well. He also discovered that they were taking the calves to a secret corral in White River Valley, where the calves were fattened to ready them for market. When the brand inspectors found the corral, it contained fifty-three long-eared Hereford calves.

At dawn on the ninth day, weapons in hand, they returned to the mountain ranch to make the arrest.

"We knew John Casey, Jr., was there—him and his wife, Alice, and this other guy. We found the woman. She come out and done everything but spit in my face. We found the other man—Barney Simpson. We couldn't find John Casey, Jr."

Shirley "took tracks." He went around the house "trying to cut his tracks, anywhere." No tracks. He made a wider circle around the house. No tracks.

"I made three circles, trying to pick up a track where he'd got out of there. He didn't get out of there. We knew he was there. We got back in and lifted up a trapdoor and found him under the floor. He wasn't armed. Barney Simpson had a gun, laying on a little nightstand there, a little stool. He reached for it. I said, 'You will die if you grab that gun.' "

Simpson elected not to die, and the two men were removed to Nye County Jail. "All we ever got Simpson and John Casey, Jr., was five years," Shirley told me ruefully. "Simpson was put on probation. We put Casey in the Nevada pen."

"**N**o godliness," Shirley said again, finishing the story. "This man John Casey, I sit in his house one day, in Little Fish Lake Valley. I was down there inspectin' cattle for him, and was washin' my face, gettin' ready to go have dinner. And he said, 'You know something?' He's layin' back on a couch—he's a big man, about six feet two. And he said, 'You know, my dad always told me, "Never make a deal that you can't make over." ' That meant he wouldn't honor a contract, or anything. He made it over. That's the way he lived. He didn't make a deal that he couldn't make over."

Marge said, "And they lived like animals. With their cute little girls."

Shirley said, "In the Kawich Mountains, in Nye County—I was down there with a federal vet—we seen this dust going up this canyon. We go up the canyon to see what's going on. There is Casey with two of his daughters —say, thirteen and fifteen, pretty little girls—and a truck backed up to a corral. The girls had had no food and were hungry. While their father was loading cattle, I handed 'em a can of peaches. When you load cattle, you know, you're right up back of 'em, poundin' 'em, tryin' to get 'em in the truck. They pooped all over him. And he got up with his pocket knife—pulled it out, and scraped it all off, and sat down, and wiped his knife, and then he opened the can of peaches and stabbed a peach and handed it to his daughters."

Shirley's roll call of rustlers includes the late Beverly Hooper, of Newark Valley, under the Diamond Range. Hooper had a corral there veneered in rustled rawhide, so that it more or less resembled a leather boxing ring. Shirley believed that Hooper was stealing cattle and selling the meat to a café in Eureka.

"He was a handsome big man, about six foot one, very intelligent, but he was a bad one, a horribly dishonest, ungodly human being. I had had him in court once—but just for selling uninspected meat was all I could get him for. It was illegal meat. I knew it was somebody else's beef. But I couldn't prove it. I had him in and got him fined a hundred and fifty bucks. You betcha. He had studied some law and was a sharp guy, for that matter, but he couldn't lay in bed straight. He had taken these hides and cut 'em to where you couldn't find the brands. To get rid of the hides, he just cut strips and wrapped his whole corral. He wrapped it around and around and around like that. In the corners he wrapped them around the other poles and made them tight. Rawhide when it dries is tight. A cow could hit that and it would not break. I went there at night—I come in out of Elko County, so they wouldn't know I was there—and I found this vantage point down to where cattle, other cattle, were mixed together. And I seen his car come around the point of the mountain over here two miles, go down into the flat. All of a sudden, I see a flash of fire, and then I heard the report of a gun, you know—so I knew they had killed something. And before long I seen 'em—with binoculars—go to the back of the car and put something in. And when they come back they didn't turn and go back to the ranch, they turned toward me. I had no place to go.

I couldn't get turned around. So I decided to tough it out. It was stupid on my part to do such a thing. Because I'm alone out there. But I had a two-way radio. When they drove up to me, I had my red light right here in a spotlight. I flipped that on. It burned out. It made one flash and burned out. So I flipped my headlights onto 'em, and I got out of the car and motioned for 'em to come back up, and I had the radio right up to my mouth and they didn't know who I was in contact with. I got 'em out of the car. Five of 'em, four men and a boy—Hooper was one of 'em. And I had 'em lay face down on the oil and keep their legs apart, and told 'em to stay where they were. And they didn't know— me with that microphone—who I was in contact with. When they seen that red light flash, they knew it was law, and they didn't know how many I had out in the brush. They didn't know that. But it was a foolish thing to have done. I had Hooper get up and open the back of the car. What did he have in there? A jackrabbit. That's all he had. I had to let him go. He had the laugh on me."

In Hamlin Valley, answering a call for help one day, Shirley picked up three long-eared calves. He later matched them to their mothers in a neutral corral. Then he and another man staked out the corral.

"We sat on 'em with a tommy gun, with a .45 automatic, waiting for the thieves to try to steal the evidence. Over Thanksgiving, we sat on 'em day and night."

One of the rustlers they caught was the deputy sheriff of Millard County, Utah.

"We put him in the penitentiary. He was a man I knew all my life. His name was Art Loper. He was a one-eyed man. He had a hell of a horse. He could rope a calf and snub 'im up tight in the saddle, you know what I mean, against his right leg, and go up to the back of a truck, and this horse would jump in and pull the calf right in the truck with him. Roan horse. Loper was trying to help feed a family. He had a big family. And there was damned poor pickin's for 'em, I'll tell you. But if he was stealin' someone else's cows he had to be stopped."

Shirley reflected for a while, and then he said, "If you run on the open range, you'd better have a brand. The law don't require you to brand anything under six months of age, no, no, but anybody in their right mind would have a recorded iron and have every animal branded, because you're asking somebody to take an oreana—you know, a long-eared critter—off from ya. I mean, if he doesn't have an iron on. Possession is nine points of the law. If you didn't catch him at it, he could steal everything you had."

Late in April, not long ago, a pickup hauling a horse trailer pulled in under the cottonwoods and the Chinese elms of Nyala, also called Cross L Ranch, where cattle are branded Cross L Combined.

$$\mathsf{t}$$

This was in Railroad Valley, which somehow seems more vast, austere, remote, silent, and empty than almost any other Nevada valley. The ranch and its range allotments measured fifteen by thirty-five miles—three hundred and thirty-six thousand acres—and many slick calves were known to be scattered about it. The ranch had a reputation for being more casual than others, unscientific. ("They let things take care of themselves.") If an animal fell dead, it might be left for some time where it was. A manure fire there had once burned for weeks. The location, even by

Nevada standards, was described as "backcountry." The trailer was sizable, and had some plywood in it and a horse. As two men got out of the pickup, they were greeted by Norman Sharp.

He had been in a hayfield when the trailer approached. He was bearded, in his fifties, patient and pleasant in manner—a bachelor, like his brother and partner Gerald. In Shirley Robison's description: "They are topnotch people. They wouldn't ship anybody else's critters for anything in the world. You betcha. They're straight as dies. No way they would take anything from anyone. They're good ranchers, in a way. I mean, they're conservative, and that's what makes them good. Makes 'em a success. They came back from almost bankruptcy after the Caseys were stealin' from 'em. They're good business people, but they've lived out in the backwoods so doggone long they're countrified."

Now, on that April day, Norman Sharp invited the two men—Leo Stewart and Wayne Lee—into his house for a glass of iced tea. The pair had been there six weeks before, when the Sharps traded them five calves for one horse. They had taken three calves. Now they had come for the two others. Tea swirling, cubes rattling, they mentioned that they would also like to trade that horse in the trailer for five more calves. If all this sounded like a Las Vegas shuffle—a way of exchanging a hundred-dollar bill for ten ones, six tens, and nine fives—it may have been. They wanted the calves for roping practice. Wayne Lee and Leo Stewart were, among other things, professional ropers. They performed together in pair roping—two against the clock, taking, say, 4.8 seconds to rope horns and then feet and have a steer stretched out. They could win as much as ten thousand dollars in such events, in Panaca or Caliente or Pioche or Ely or Tonopah—wherever the little rodeos would be.

Norman Sharp—in his denim, his suspenders, his

grange demeanor—thought that Wayne Lee had "a touch of the slick" about him, that "he looked like a cowboy." Lee was lean, tall, rough, and rugged-looking, in the potato-chip hat, the Levi's, the boots, and the spurs. His belt buckle was inlaid with silver and gold. He made his home in Las Vegas.

Leo Stewart's buckle was also inlaid with silver and gold, but he was from Alamo, in Lincoln County, and he looked more like a farmer—like Gordon Eldridge or, for that matter, Norman Sharp. The son of a range cowboy, he was huskier and shorter than Wayne Lee. He was red-faced, heavy-jowled, quiet, and friendly. The two had been partners scarcely six months.

Lee was a breaker of horses. Large letters on the gooseneck trailer said "WAYNE LEE HORSE TRAINING." He was a second cousin of Shirley Robison's colleague Arshal Lee, and as descendants of John D. Lee they belonged to one of the first families of the Great Basin. Their distinguished forebear had participated in the murder of the occupants of an emigrant wagon train in what historians call the Mountain Meadows massacre. Of Wayne Lee's several occupations, the primary one was breaking, gentling, and training horses. But he also held still another job, even more pertinent to this story. He worked for the State of Nevada under the supervision of Chris Collis. He was a deputy brand inspector.

Norman Sharp had a good opinion of Wayne Lee as a trainer, but he rode the horse that had come in the trailer and said he was not interested in making the trade.

"It's a broke horse, a good horse."

"No, not at this time, thank you. It needs more training to be worth the price of five one-year-old heifers."

The two calves that the Sharps owed to Stewart and Lee were in a corral. They were Herefords, the only breed the Sharps run, and, like nearly all Cross L Ranch calves, they were small for their age, with good heavy horns, and hair lighter than most Herefords'. Before they could go, they would require brand inspection. "We'll get Carl Hanks to do it," Norman said, mentioning a deputy brand inspector who lived not far up the valley.

Wayne Lee said, "We don't need him. I can do it." He soon handed Sharp a brand-inspection certificate for the two calves, naming Stewart as the buyer. While he and Stewart were putting the calves into the trailer with the horse, one calf got away. In 4.8 seconds plus a couple of minutes on either side, they had roped the calf and hauled it to the trailer. When they departed, they had been at Nyala two hours.

They went off to the southwest about twenty miles, their dust out of sight over the curve of the earth, and then they headed east toward the mountains, still on allotted Cross L range. Beside a deep wash under high red bluffs, they climbed the mountain bench on a two-rut road, passing any number of Cross L cow/calf pairs. They went high, near the roadhead, turned around in the brush, and backed into a smaller wash, where they parked and took the horse out of the trailer. If they had started roping at the bottom, they would have driven cattle above them up and out of the country.

One of them mounted the horse and went up into the brush northwest, where he threw his loop and a calf crashed on its side, into the black sage. Over the gravelly ground they hauled it to the trailer, and used a lot of muscle forcing it in. Then one man stayed with the truck while the other rode downhill to rope a second calf. Truck and trailer joined the scene. There was another big scuffle as the calf was pulled to the road.

They were not heeling the calves, and heaven knows

they weren't fishing for them. They were roping them around the horns or the neck. In Chris Collis's words, "You rope around the horns, the cow will go better. You get closer. You take your dallies, and you drag that steer where you want him to go. Roping them around the neck, you shut off their air and they go down."

The most difficult animal was roped in the black sage near an overtowering butte. It was not about to be dragged to the road, so they drove the trailer through the brush some hundreds of yards to get it. In this manner, calf after calf, they packed the trailer as they worked their way downhill. To the west-northwest they could see fifty miles to the Monitor Range—over intervening summits and, in the foreground, the immense treeless valley. There was a big dry lake bed, white, in the valley. In all that landscape they could see no sign of as much as one human being; and, as far as is known, no one observed them. Nor did they ever tell this story. After shoving the horse in among the calves, and obscuring the nature of their cargo with plywood, they left, along the bench, on the rarely travelled road to the south.

After a time, a plume of dust belonging to Gerald Sharp came up the same road in the opposite direction. Gerald had been running an errand, and had passed Lee's rig, and now, along the escarpment near a water hole called Eds Well, he saw tire tracks on a spur that climbed the bench toward Red Bluff Spring. Minutes later, at Nyala, Norman told him about Lee and Stewart's visit.

"How long ago did they leave?" Gerald asked.

Norman said, "Six hours."

Wayne Lee was interesting but incidental—a late-appearing walk-on with spurs. If there was one rustler that

Chris Collis had ever hoped to convict, it was Leo Stewart, this quiet unpretentious roper with, as Chris put it, "a reputation that wouldn't quit"—a man suspected of so much cattle theft that Chris eventually kept an eight-by-ten color picture of him as a souvenir. From the day that Shirley Robison retired and Chris assumed the title of District Brand Inspector, he was beset with complaints, hearsay, suspicions, and innuendo coming at him from all directions about Leo Stewart; yet, if all these things were true, the evidence was cunningly kept beyond reach, and years went by while Chris waited for an unambiguous chance.

The Sharps, for their part, "for years and years" had thought that Stewart looked upon them as prey. Their Cross L Combined brand had much in common with the H Over L used at that time by one of Stewart's relatives, and even more in common with H Hanging L Combined, which he could easily pass off as his relative's brand. Looking at these brands, in that order, one could almost see a scribe bent over his table in Beijing building a composite character.

The Sharps had attempted to collect evidence and deal with Stewart on their own—in part because they looked upon him as a friend—but they had failed. Their fiscal blood count was once again turning white. Exasperated, they agreed to call the brand inspector. Lacking a telephone, as they still do, they would have to use one that was twenty-five miles away.

Next morning, soon after daybreak, Gerald drove there, and called Chris in Ely. Anxious not to reveal his purpose to anyone listening in, Gerald kept his voice slow, flat, and detached. He didn't say why he was asking Chris to come and visit. Chris knew where the phone was, sensed urgency, and departed for Nyala.

When a brand inspector writes a certificate, he draws a slanting line through any unused space, closing the certificate, and limiting it to the listed cattle. He collects money and sends the white original to the state. A yellow copy stays in his certificate book, a blue one goes to the buyer, and a pink one to the seller. At Nyala, as the Sharps told him their story, they showed him the pink certificate written by Wayne Lee to cover the calves they owed him. In one glance, Chris saw less than he needed to know but more than enough to make him active. There was no slanting line. There was free space for additional entries. Not drawing the line is known as "leaving it open."

With Gerald, he went down the bench to Eds Well, but when he saw the multiwheeled tracks going into and coming out of the brush, and "the horseshoe prints in the dirt where the horse was pulling something heavy," and the story of roping and loading written into the sage, he decided to go no farther. "The chain of evidence has to be maintained or the evidence is no good," he explains. To read and record tracks and sign as thoroughly as possible, he wanted another pair of professional eyes to go with him into the brush. He called the Nevada Division of Investigations and, within a few hours, was joined by an agent named Steve Nevin.

Chris rode on the hood of Nevin's pickup as they climbed the mountain bench at a rate that could have been reckoned in yards per hour. Where he signalled, they stopped. They made notes and photographs. They collected and labelled tufts of hair. They picked up the story from the end to the beginning, working on the last roping first, and then moving uphill to the penultimate roping, and so on, in order not to risk obscuring things with their own equipment. From the manner in which treads covered treads they could read the directions in which the truck-and-trailer had moved. The horse-trailer tracks were "shallow going up, coming back they were real deep." When Nevin's pickup came to a place where a calf had been roped or where the trailer had been stopped and loaded, Chris could see what had happened: "You could see where the calf crushed the sage. There was red hair on the brush. Where the gravelly ground was really disturbed, you could tell it was a calf, roped. There were scuff marks all over the road where a calf balked getting in." All were Hereford calves. At each place where the trailer had been opened, hay and manure had fallen out in a straight line. This was not in summer dust. The moisture of an April rain, a few days old, added clarity to the tracks and to Steve Nevin's photographs. "I don't claim to be a real good tracker," Chris says. With a short pause for reconsideration, he continues, "Well, I read tracks pretty good. When I see them, it's as if somebody turned on a light switch." He could see the size of each animal roped and removed. He could see the roper, after roping a calf, "take a few dallies and maneuver the calf onto its feet and to the road—either one of them could do it." The narrative of the calf ropings by Lee and Stewart in Red Bluff Canyon would derive entirely from this investigation, which continued into the next day. The highest line of hay and manure that Nevin and Collis found was in the wash where Lee and Stewart had removed the horse from the trailer.

The rustled cattle could have been taken (1) who knows where, (2) to Stewart's place, in Alamo, (3) to Lee's, in Las Vegas. Chris had to make a quick decision and go. Stewart was the ranking rustler, Lee the neophyte, he reasoned, but Stewart was also a cattle rancher with plenty of roping calves, while Lee not only had no ranch but was not even from Nevada. He was, as Nevadans see it, from Las Vegas, a foreign country. "I just know we'll find 'em there," Chris said. "If we're lucky, we'll find his brand-inspection book there, too."

Lee lived on Rosada in northwest Vegas. In corrals there Collis and Nevin saw, from the street, about a dozen Hereford calves, small for their age, with good heavy horns, and hair lighter than most Herefords'. They soon returned with a search warrant, a gooseneck trailer, and a black-and-white unit. In a black-and-white unit, a cop is behind the wheel. Lee was in Fallon at a roping. His brand-inspection-certificate book was in a vinyl briefcase on the dining table. Lee had added ten animals to the certificate left open at Nyala. In the corrals outside, all the calves were freshly branded.

Chris hardly needed to refer to his book. Lazy H Seven Combined was registered in the name of Leo Stewart, Alamo, Nevada 89001. Chris loaded the calves into the trailer and followed the black-and-white unit into downtown Las Vegas. Before he left Railroad Valley, he had told Carl Hanks to go up to Red Bluff Spring and gather tight-bagged cows. Hanks had gathered three. After seeing the calves at Lee's, Chris had called Hanks and told him to take the cows to Horseman's Park in Las Vegas, where Clark County Animal Control had some holding corrals. In the dark of evening, he was now headed for the park himself with the impounded calves, and the heavy traffic was confusing, the noise intense, the lights of the casinos chatoyant. At the park, a horse show was under way in blazing light. This was close to Sam's Town, the big casino. "Imagine cows in downtown Las Vegas. They had never been hauled before. The cattle were stressed. The truck ride had been a shock to the animals' systems. They were older calves. Turned into the holding corrals, they were running, trying to leave, hitting fences. You could just not expect a normal mothering-up response." And none came when cows and calves were placed together.

At each stop in Vegas, almost everyone he encountered was a friend of Wayne Lee. The warmest greeting he received was "You better be sure. You better know what you're doing." Then, slowly, in the dead of night, the animals calmed down, and so did the turgid city. In the morning, two of the three big-bag cows had been sucked. The teats were clean. The hair around the bags was curly. The bags were no longer tight. It wasn't a sprawl of evidence, covering countless examples, but it would do. If your game is icebergs, you might have to settle for tips.

Stewart and Lee pleaded not guilty. Theirs was the longest criminal trial in the history of Nye County. Chris was on the stand for four days. The defense said it was not possible to rope more than one calf in two hours. Lee and Stewart were convicted on five counts of grand larceny of cattle. Each was fined sixteen thousand dollars. Each got twenty-five years, but the judge put them on probation and did not send them up. Chris slowly shakes his hat as he finishes the story, saying, "They were convicted on grand larceny and spent not one day in jail."

While I'm out with Chris in the basins and ranges on his long, unplanned rounds, we find ourselves on a small dirt road in Railroad Valley, heading north. "Was this the road that Lee and Stewart used?" I ask him.

The muffler comes loose under the state pickup. It falls, one end clanging. He stops, gets out, looks at the muffler, and hunts the bed of the pickup for baling wire. In several hundred square miles of sage basin and rising ground, no structure is in sight to any horizon. "Not this road," he answers. "They were travelling the backcountry."

He secures the muffler and drives on. Baling wire, he informs me, is Mormon buckskin. We stop in at Nyala, an authentic oasis. Karen Uhalde grew up just across the eastern mountains, and went to high school with Chris in Ely, a hundred and twelve miles north. The Sharps' ranch has the waste-nothing aspect of bush Alaska. All about in deep profusion are tractors, swathers, choppers, feed wagons, dump wagons, a corn harvester, a baler, a combine, stock trucks, a welder, a cement truck, old disks, plows, land planes, an old pump jack, irrigation pipe, sprinkling equipment, wheel-line parts, gated pipes, siphoning tubes, corrugators, markers, and seed drills. In the background are great mounds of hay, quonsets of hay. Norman and Gerald Sharp, their brother Melvin, their sister Marian, and her husband, Ed Ylst, nod to Chris and swiftly form a huddle around me, in which they let me know without ambiguity that the federal government is an almost pure evil. I sense, in the huddle, that I am standing in for the federal government. Compared with the federal government, moreover, they'd call Leo Stewart the lesser rustler. "Leo had been a problem since he was fifteen," Norman says. "For him, rustling was a way of life, not a necessity. Some people steal because they're hungry. Others for a lark. And for a third group it's a way of life. If it wasn't for Chris, they could come in to the desert here, load up, and be in Kansas in a few days. Both Lee and Stewart were good ropers. They probably met at a roping show. It isn't a closed society. In Nevada, if you don't know someone, you know about them. Leo and Wayne had been here. Strange as it may seem, you know they're doing this, but they're still friends. Leo is not an unlikable person. But when they start doing it every three weeks you know it's a business. If I stood on your toe, you might tolerate it for a while, but eventually you say, 'Enough of this shit.' "

Soon after daybreak on a cold October morning, sprinkler fields are frozen in Steptoe Valley. We go south and past them to Three C Ranch. This is private pasture, some thousands of acres, where the basin is no more than ten miles wide, gently concave under the fans of its flanking ranges. There's an eight-foot fence to keep elk out—also antelope and mountain sheep. Far out there in the deepest ground—in the axis of the valley, collected—are fourteen hundred head of cattle. Half are about to go east. The ranch belongs to Bidart Brothers, a company in California. The brand is the Long Tail B.

B

The cattle, massed and choral, are a mile away—a unit slowly seething, now to the left, now to the right, with dust around them, among them, above them, like fog. Four cowboys on horseback and one in a pickup are trying to move them into a long fenced lane that comes up to the corrals. Their sound, in its concentration, is orchestral, and large in volume despite the distance. The punctuating soloists, whose contributions would be prominent nearby, are blended into the total vibration. If you could not see the animals, you would not know what you were hearing. They sound like baritone whales. They sound like jets passing overhead without Doppler effect. They sound like an all-tuba band warming up. They seem to be creating the serious music of the twenty-first century.

"Too many cows and not enough cowboys," Chris remarks as we wait. When the cattle finally begin to move toward us, they stop, jam, rebel, retreat, and start again. A dart leader goes out in front, and the rest follow for a hundred yards, but then they stop, jam, struggle backward. "They hesitate coming up the lane because they turn around looking for their calves," he explains. "When they hear calves bawling, they stop and look for their own. If you rope a calf and drag it in front of them, they'll follow."

The cowboys shout. They pop their chaps with their romals. On their heads are baseball caps. As they draw close to the corrals, in the oncoming rise of dust, we can hear the *patrón* switching from Spanish to English to Spanish. His name is Melchor Gragirena. The cowboys tie their horses to a fence of the outermost corral and work the cattle forward on foot. This is a complex of large rectangular corrals flanked on two sides by an alley. With their stock whips in motion, fast on their feet, they move the cattle up the alley and separate cows from heifers from steers. To the greatest extent possible, they try to be gingerly and calm. "The least amount of working, the least shrink," Chris remarks. The calves are on their way to a scale. Shrink is loss of weight, up to and for the most part including manure. The calves here will be worth about a third of a million dollars. In one sudden burst of fear and flight, they can leave a thousand dollars on the ground.

Cows go into one corral, heifers next door. Steers remain in the sorting alley. Ingenious combinations of swinging gates make it possible to separate cows from calves and sex the calves at the same time. A lot of ranches do not have

such facilities, and have to run their calves a second time
to sex them, resulting in more shrink.

Chris is in the alley counting. He is up against the fence
as the steers race past him, and he writes with a pen on the
palm of his hand. He is facing east, into the early sun,
because the Long Tail B is on the right ribs and the steers
are running to his right. There is no adjusting these less
than ideal factors. I have watched him inspecting cattle in
a large, rectangular mountain corral where he took a position with his back to the sun while a cowboy sent before
him, clockwise, a stream of calves branded on their left hips.
(The cowboy, in fringed-buckskin chaps, was a moonlight-
ing Baptist minister.) Now, in this confining alley, Chris is
compelled to squint, but he can see the Long Tail B, even
if I cannot. The steer calves look slick to me—most of them,
anyway—while Chris seems to have electronic eyes that are
reading hair-covered bar codes. He assembles the steers in
groups of eighteen, recording their numbers on his skin.
He says, "I use a lot of three-by-five cards when I run out
of space on my hand."

The female calves, in their corral next to the alley, have
spontaneously lined up in ranks, shoulder to shoulder, ignored for the moment and suddenly placid, staring toward
the alley with their grandmotherly, contemplative eyes.
Brockle-faced heifers, coon-eyed heifers, redneck heifers
(the touch of Angus), they are learning a lot in a hurry. The
dust is so dense it tastes. From the cows' corral comes a din
of foghorns.

Cows are mounting cows in the cows' corral. Roan
cows. Brockle-faced cows. Hundreds of cows are crowded
together, wailing, crying, sobbing, bawling—and riding one
another. The hair is wet on the calves' noses in the alley
and the heifer pen, so recently have they been sucking.

Among them there seem to be no dogies—leppies, orphans.

Chris flicks his fingers as he counts the running steers, as if he were shaking off water. *"Diez y seis!"* he calls to a cowboy. The cowboy nods. As the steers approach, Chris first checks the ears. The right ears have been marked by being halved down the middle. (The heifers' right ears are notched.) He checks also for strings—the long strands of dangling hair that are the only sign that a calf is male. Then he looks for the brands as the animals pass him. He looks again at the ears when they have gone by. He writes with a ballpoint. His hands—palms and backs—are now covered with ink. Why does he write on his hands? "It's easier. *Diez y siete! Diez y ocho!*" The cowboy shuts a gate. Chris opens another gate, and the steers, en bloc, go onto the scale: seven thousand five hundred and eleven pounds at ninety-seven cents a pound.

I have two apples in my pocket. Does he want one?

"No, thanks!" he shouts. "I've got a mouthful of Copenhagen!" He lives on Copenhagen, by his own description. He has nothing but coffee in the morning. He seems to forget to eat lunch. There's a circular protuberance in his shirt pocket, in his jaw a pillow of snuff.

Now, in the alley, he is stopping six, his legs in the shuffle of defense. Like a basketball player, he has moved on experience and without thinking—because his glance has fallen upon an underbit in one calf's ear. He separates her from the steers.

A slick bull calf shows up in the alley—born too late for the branding. Chris cuts him out, too.

Cattle are auctioned by satellite now, in truckload units of fifty thousand pounds—but few from Nevada. The buyer has a dish antenna, and sits at home watching videotaped cattle in the egret flats of Alvin, Texas, on the Red River plain of Louisiana, against the velvet greens of Jane Lew,

West Virginia, and back to the pastures of Easterly, Texas, where mahogany steers against a stand of trees are up to their hocks in grass. "They walk on more feed than these cattle out here get a chance to look at," Chris remarked one afternoon when we were watching his set. It's not a bad way to see the country, four hours, coast to coast, cow to cow—in one afternoon, thirteen million five hundred thousand dollars' worth of cattle sold. In this part of Nevada, more often than not, the middleman is Denny Manzonie—order buyer, livestock dealer, broker—who buys cattle, takes them to his lots in Nye County, and resells them to many forms of client, from other ranchers to Super Fresh and Foodtown. Lacking a personal satellite, Manzonie is, in his words, "busier than a fart in a skillet."

Six big semis have come to the Three C. They are eighteen-wheelers, made of aluminum to improve the weight ratio of cattle to truck. They are multilevelled and multichambered. You can get fifty thousand pounds of living beef into an extremely small space, as Delta once whispered to United. More than a hundred and fifty tons of calf are ready for the semis now. After the scale, they enter still another corral, next door to their bawling mothers. Their destination is Wilsey, Kansas, which impresses the brand inspector, who says, "They're really going east."

He counts them all again as they are loading. They go up a chute in eights and tens, balking, twisting, sometimes forcing their way back, and the truck drivers lean over the side of the chute holding four-cell electric prods. The prods are now and again effective, but less so than the brand inspector, who closes a small gate at the bottom of the ramp and follows each pulse of cattle upward, leaning hard into them with one shoulder, his legs driving.

"I've seen inspectors who don't get out of the pickup," a truck driver remarks.

The calves, six and eight months old and averaging four hundred pounds, back down on the brand inspector and pin him against the gate. They seem to be crushing him, but he muscles back, shouts "Hey hey hey hey hey, calves!" and piercingly whistles through his teeth. They turn and climb for Kansas.

"A lot of brand inspectors sit on the fences, but it makes a long day," he has said to me. "It's just something I've chose not to do. If you're going to do that, there's no sense to even go."

A hundred and sixteen climb into the first truck, a hundred and twenty-six into the second. After the door closes on the seven-hundred-and-fifth calf, he writes his brand certificate, and collects the four hundred and twenty-three dollars he has earned for the State of Nevada. The trucks are free to go. In the cow corral, the sound is more intense than ever. Weaning by semi. The sound of the gears is lost in the din as the semis pull away.

The cows are released from their corral and allowed to mill about. They are not driven back to the fenced and distant pastures. They would break down fences to get back to the corrals where their calves were shipped. Tomorrow, beside the corrals the powder will be a foot deep as cattle walk the fence line looking for their calves.

[*Brands drawn by Ellie Wyeth Fox*]

RELEASE

.

In Lancaster, Pennsylvania, some years ago, I met a pure humanist whose spirit had prospered with the rise of technology. His name was Robert Russell. For several decades, he had been a professor at Franklin and Marshall College, taking his rotations as chairman of the English Department, and writing, meanwhile, innumerable articles and several books. "Previously, writing was not a solitary enterprise for me," he remarked, turning away from his computer. "On the typewriter, I could do a draft by myself, but it would be a terrible mess, technically, because I couldn't remember what I had written. If I was interrupted by a telephone call—or if my mind wandered—I would forget what I had last said. And unless I got hold of somebody and asked what I had said—asked, for example, 'Where am I? Did I make a space after the s of fish, or did I put the h there? Should I do a backspace h to make fish?'—unless I could depend on somebody else to find that sort of thing, I'd just have to plunge ahead and hope."

Russell's computer was an I.B.M. PC upgraded to the level of an XT with a twenty-megabyte hard disk. His fingers flew about the keyboard, and green words leaped to the screen:

> There once was a pony named Lucius
> Whose mother was owne by Confucius;
> He won all the races
> In mountainous places
> Except for the Prix-de-Vesuvius.

The room, under eaves, had no windows. On the walls were a stuffed hawk, an inscribed and framed poem by Stanley Kunitz, and a couple of aerial lithographs of Oxford University—courts and quadrangles that Russell had inhabited but had never seen. On his desk was a Perkins Brailler, with platform spacebar and spatulate keys, looking embarrassed in the presence of the computer. I remarked that there was a typo in the limerick and wondered (aloud) how much time would be required for Russell to find it. The answer was ten seconds—after he touched the F6 key and his machine began to talk:

> There once was a punny named Loose ee us

In every respect—from its black-and-cream façade to its hopping dance of green words—the computer was identical to its I.B.M. peers, with one exception. A small box called ECHO GP, connected by a wire to a card of chips inside, was prepared to recite the words on the screen. Its accent, as one might expect, was hard to place. It verged on dialect. Deep, nasal, reverberant, tympanic, it was the voice of an extraterrestrial who had acquired a job in a large city announcing the departure of trains.

> Whose mother was owne by Con foo see us

"Something wrong there," Russell remarked, and he put in the missing d.

"How did you know?"

"Just by listening. It said own but not deh."

The machine's pronunciation was generally intelligible but frequently outlandish.

He won all the ray sez
In moun tane us play sez
Except for the pricks . . .

Russell compared understanding it to understanding French. As he went on to demonstrate the composition of fresh prose—writing sentences, correcting them, rearranging words and phrases—the thing said hee vee for heavy, lee den for leaden, hor ee zun for horizon, and soul derr for solder. Baseball was base a ball. Chin ease was an Asian people. The voice articulated all punctuation: "semi collon . . . comma . . . point." At the ends of lines it said "ree turn." It could speak whole lines forwards or backwards, or speak one word and stop. With the touch of other keys, it would articulate a letter at a time, in either direction. At the end of a file, it said, "end of doc u ment, end of doc u ment." It was not incapable of annoying Russell.

He won all the ray sez ree turn
In moun tane us play sez ree turn
Except for the pricks minus-de-minus Veh soo
    vee us point end of doc u ment end of doc u ment
    end of doc u ment

"Oh, shut up!" Russell instructed it, and he hit Alt N. "With Alt N, I can shut him up," he said. "I'm sick of him.

He bores me." The voice spent some time in the slammer. Then Russell hit Alt R to bring it back.

Writing another sentence, he put into the computer the coined word skglytijghstehfyt. When the voice reached it, the voice made no attempt to pronounce it, but equably said, "S k g l y t i j g h s t e h f y t."

"It accepts what I do and tries to deal with it," Russell said. "Because it doesn't know."

"It doesn't know from nothin'," I agreed. "It's a blank sheet of paper."

"Yeah. It doesn't know that skglytijghstehfyt isn't a word. But it says to itself, *'He's* supposed to know. I'll just spell that back to him, and if he makes sense out of it, fine. I don't make any sense out of it, but then I'm only a computer.' "

Bob Russell was then sixty-two—compact, fine-featured, Celtic in demeanor, his hair a thickish gray brush-cut. He antedated the tape recorder, the electric typewriter. He found an old croquet mallet when he was five, and pounded it on a concrete walk to secure the head. The brittle wood shattered, and a sharp point entered the pupil of his left eye. Attempts to save the eye led to an infection that spread sympathetically to the other eye. He lost all vision. He was the youngest of seven children, son of a shopkeeper in Binghamton who sold jewelry and men's clothing. Aged six, he entered the New York Institute for the Education of the Blind, 999 Pelham Parkway, the Bronx. Most of his classmates went home on weekends. He was from so far away that he went home three times a year. He learned the IRT by the lurch of the curve, the pitch of the screaming metal, the relationship of platforms to doors. On the streets of Manhattan, he sought pizza with his nose. On the school's athletic field, he learned to scoop up a football from the sound of the bounce. He became an accomplished wrestler.

In a three-sided courtyard, he played a version of base-ball in which the student who served as umpire was frequently told he was "blind as a bat." Russell pulls out these stories like bottles of wine in a book called "To Catch an Angel."

When Russell was twelve, his brother James sent him a Remington portable with a note that said he would have to learn how to use it if he was to progress in school. The work that he did on the Remington carried him to Hamilton College, and on, transferring, to Yale, where he was a varsity wrestler, and to England—B.Litt. (Oxon.). Writing his last exam in his senior year in New Haven, he typed twelve pages about the Age of Johnson. This was in response to questions posed by the great Chauncey Brewster Tinker, the sound of whose name would cause a parrot to say "Yale." The Remington's ribbon got stuck on page 3. The keys broke through the cloth. Russell turned in the finished exam not knowing that nine pages were blank. When Chauncey Brewster Tinker touched the backs of the pages, he felt raised impressions that resembled Braille. He went straight to Russell's room and asked him just to recount what the exam had meant to say.

For all Russell's academic accomplishments, when he said he wanted to become a college professor he was advised repeatedly to give up the ambition. "People said to me, 'Go back to weaving baskets. You can't teach.' " He collected hundreds of polite notes in response to applications. After Yale and before Oxford, he finally got a job at Triple Cities College. The school was desperate. An alien who had been hired there had lost his birth certificate and couldn't get into the country. (Triple Cities College is now SUNY Binghamton.)

At Oxford, Russell married one of his readers, a student named Elisabeth Shaw, who had spent her early years in the Orkneys. She was to become head of the English Department at Elizabethtown College, twenty miles from Franklin and Marshall. Her late brother Robert Shaw was the writer who moonlighted as an actor in such films as "Jaws" and "The Sting." After Bob and Elisabeth Russell came to the United States, he was rejected by two hundred colleges and schools, and perforce he went to work in what he calls a "blind workshop" in Binghamton, where he literally put nuts on bolts for a year—until he was hired by Shimer College, in Mount Carroll, Illinois.

There, in 1953, he bought a Hermes 6000. He explains, "I thought it was time to move up in the technology. The Hermes had a better touch. It felt solid. By comparison, my old Remington was airborne, spongy. I had come to believe that all mechanical things are eternal, but they are not. We had a 1939 Ford that was driving the point home." By 1955, his work on the Hermes had attracted Franklin and Marshall, one of the oldest and best colleges in the United States. His ascent in technology accelerated there. "In 1966, I went up to the best thing that God had ever invented for a writer—the I.B.M. Selectric. You just touched it, and the key hit perfectly. My wife no longer had to say to me, 'You're not hitting your periods, you're not hitting your a's hard enough.' "

God, obviously, wasn't satisfied, and it took Him less than twenty years to get Russell into computers. To watch Russell at work, writing, may be the closest thing to a miracle I have ever seen. Like bouncing footballs, like the feet of approaching wrestlers, words travel every which way and he knows where they are. "I've got to have another word," he will say, revising. "That one doesn't sound right." The machine makes it possible for him to revise things without troubling someone else. Manuscript in hand, he used to say to Elisabeth, "When can you do this?" They had four children. If they were at their summer cottage (on an island in the St. Lawrence River), they would lock the doors while they worked, so the children would play inside and not go out and drown. If they were in Lancaster, Elisabeth would say, "After the kids go to bed." Reading to him what he had written, she would write down his corrections, and then she would dictate the revised version to him as he retyped it. She did not know how to type.

"I was indecisive," he told me. "And she just was incredibly patient. That's a terrible thing to subject someone to—an invasion of her time. She's got her own career, and I'm not calling on that now. I don't think I should. I don't think I ever should have, but I had no alternative. It was a terrible dependence, largely on her patience and good humor, and it was also a tension for me to be trying to write under those circumstances." There were moments when Elisabeth felt the magnetism of an imagined revision that did not and would not occur to him. This he found irritating, and the irritation in turn brought down about him a cloud of rarefied guilt. "The machine doesn't argue," he said to me with pleasure. If it did, he could hit it with Alt N.

"I can get up in the morning and work on something," he continued. "I don't have to wake anybody. The machine is always ready to be awakened. It doesn't mind changing and rechanging and changing back, changing again, changing back, back and forth. I can do this myself. And I can catch most—though not all—of the errors. It's a release, a marvelous release. A writer tries to cast an image of the mind in operation. It's a very complicated business, and best done by oneself." Now, after thirty-five years, Elisabeth will often see a piece of his for the first time when it arrives in the mail in print.

As Russell started a new file, his machine said to him, "You may be jinn typing." His word-processing software was called Qwerty, out of Danbury, New Hampshire, and its tapping cane was Soft Vert, out of Mountain View, California—a program designed to make other programs speak.

"Vert makes Qwerty vocable," Russell said. "Is that a word—vocable?"

"You may be jinn typing."

Vocable it may have been, but Vert was also idiosyncratic. It rhymed laughter with daughter. It said began like an Oxford don but it didn't know how to be jinn. As if to taunt it, Russell wrote:

It's time for my dream girl to begin dreaming.

And Soft Vert said:

It's time for my dream jirl to be jinn dreaming.

I asked Russell to write "Begin the Beguine."

"Cole Porter," he said. "How do you spell Cole? C o l l? C o l e? I'm a very bad speller. When I was a kid and read Braille, I could spell. In college, there were too many books. I'm a pitifully slow reader. I had to junk Braille, and listen to people reading. I never learned to read properly with Braille. So when it comes to a name like Cole or a word like solder, I don't have an image in my head to re-create on the page." Touching the computer, he added, "I've got a Random House dictionary in here but I don't know how to get it to talk properly."

With some help in the spelling, he typed:

Cole Porter rewrote "Begin the Beguine"

The machine said:

Cole Porter roo rote "Be jinn the Big Wine"

"Oh, shut up," Russell said. Then, tactfully—as if suddenly concerned for the feelings of a companion—he remarked, "French doesn't sound funny when you know how to speak French."

He then typed out a line of great challenge to Soft Vert:

I was tough enough though through with it.

The sentence had three different sounds in its o u g h's, and the machine pronounced them flawlessly.

Russell asked if I remembered George Bernard Shaw's essay on the anomalies of the spelling of English.

I said I did.

He asked if I remembered how Shaw spelled fish.

"G h o t i," I said. "The g and h as in laughter. The o as in women. The t and i as in nation."

Russell wrote on his computer:

Ghoti.

And the thing said:

Fish.

IN

VIRGIN

FOREST

.

In virgin forest, the ground is uneven, dimpled with mounds and adjacent pits. Perfect trees rise, yes, with boles clear to fifty and sixty feet; but imperfect trees are there, too—bent twigs, centuries after the bending—not to mention the dead standing timber, not to mention four thousand board feet rotting as one trunk among the mayapples and the violets: a toppled hull fruited with orange-and-cream fungi, which devour the wood, metabolize it, cause it literally to disappear. In virgin forest, the classic symbol of virginity is a fallen uprooted trunk decaying in a bed of herbs.

In eastern America, the primeval forest would include grapes, their free-floating vines descending like bridge cables. Wild grapes are incapable of climbing the trunks of large trees. They are lifted by trees as the trees grow, and their bunches hang from the top of the canopy. In eastern America, there is a great scarcity of virgin forest. Cut the grapevines, make a few stumps, let your cattle in to graze, and it's all over till the end of time. Nonetheless, I've been in such a place, and did not have to travel far to see it. Never cut, never turned, it was a piece of American deciduous forest in continuous evolution dating to the tundras of mesolithic time. Some of the trees were ninety feet tall, with redtails nesting in them, and when the hawks took off and rose above the canopy they could see the World Trade Center.

Franklin Township, New Jersey, includes New Brunswick and is one of the less virgin milieus in America. This is where the megalopolis came in so fast it trapped animals between motels. It missed, though, half a mile of primeval woods. The property, a little east of East Millstone, was settled in 1701 by Mynheer Cornelius VanLiew and remained in one family for two hundred and fifty-four years. They cleared and farmed most of their land but consciously decided to leave sixty-five acres untouched. The Revolution came and went, the Civil and the World Wars, but not until the nineteen-fifties did the family seek the counsel of a sawyer. The big trees were ruled by white oaks, dating to the eighteenth and seventeenth centuries, and their value was expressible in carats. Being no less frank than Dutch, the family let its intentions be known. As often will happen in conservation crises, this brought forth a paradox of interested parties: rod-and-gun groups, the Nature Conservancy, the Adirondack Mountain Club, the United Daughters of the Confederacy. A tract of virgin forest is so rare that money was raised in thirty-eight states and seven foreign countries. But not enough. The trees were worth a good deal more. In the end, the forest was saved by, of all people, the United Brotherhood of Carpenters and Joiners of America, whose president remarked in 1955, as he handed over the property to Rutgers University, "What happens in the woodlands is close to the carpenter's heart."

Named for a brotherhood president, the tract is called

Hutcheson Memorial Forest. A brief trail makes a loop near one end. The deed limits Rutgers to that, and Rutgers is not arguing. The university's role is to protect the periphery and to study the woods. When something attacks, Rutgers makes notes. A disease that kills American beeches is on its way from Maine. "The forest deed says basically you don't do anything about it, you watch what happens," a biologist named Edmund Stiles explained. A few years ago, gypsy moths tore off the canopy and sunlight sprayed the floor. The understory thickened, as shrubs and saplings responded with a flush of growth. "The canopy is now closing over again," Stiles said. "This summer, there will be a lot of death." In 1950, a hurricane left huge gaps in the canopy. "Once every three hundred years you can expect a hurricane that will knock down damned near everything," Stiles went on. "There's a real patchwork nature in an old forest, in the way it is always undergoing replacement." He stopped to admire a small white ash standing alone beneath open sky. "That's going to take the canopy," he said. "It's going to go all the way. It has been released. It will fill the gap."

Forty-two years old and of middle height—wearing boots, blue jeans, a brown wool shirt—Stiles had a handsome set of mutton chops and a tumble of thick brown hair that flowed over his forehead toward inquiring blue eyes. He had been working in Hutcheson Forest for thirteen years, and had recently become director. His doctoral dissertation, at the University of Washington, was on bird communities in alder forests. More recently, he had studied the foraging strategies of insects and the symbiotic relationships of berries and migratory birds. In other words, he was a zoologist and a botanist, too. From secretive gray foxes to the last dead stick—that was what the untouched forest was about. The big oaks (red, white, and black), the shagbark hickories, sugar maples, beeches, ashes, and dogwoods—among thousands of plant and animal species—were only the trees.

As we talked, and moved about, tasting the odd spice-bush leaf or a tendril of smilax, Stiles divided his attention and seemed not to miss a sound. "Spicebush and dogwood fruits are very high in lipids," he said. "They are taken on by birds getting ready for long migratory flights. Those are wood thrushes calling. A forest has to be at least a hundred years old to get a wood thrush. Actually, it takes about four centuries to grow a forest of this kind. The gap phenomenon is typical of old forest. There's a white-eyed vireo. Blue-winged warbler. There are cycles of openness and closedness in the canopies. Trees take advantage. Fill in the gaps. These are white-oak seedlings from a mast year. There's a nice red-bellied woodpecker." He was like Toscanini, just offstage, listening idly to his orchestra as it tuned itself up. He said he had developed a theory that out-of-season splotches of leaf color are messages to frugivorous birds—the scattered early orange among sassafras leaves, the springtime red of the leaves of the wild strawberry, the red of the Virginia creeper when everything else is green. When fruit is ready, the special colors turn on. He heard a great-crested flycatcher. He bent down to a jack-in-the-pulpit, saying that it bears bird-disseminated fruit and is pollinated by a small black fly.

German foresters who had come to visit Hutcheson Forest had been surprised by the untidiness of the place, startled by the jumble of life and death. "These Germans are unfamiliar with stuff just lying around, with the truly virginal aspect of the forest," Stiles said. Apparently, the Germans, like almost everyone else, had a misconception of forest primeval—a picture of Wotan striding through the noonday twilight, of Ludwig D. Boone shouting for

Lebensraum among giant columns of uniform trees. "You don't find redwoods," Stiles remarked summarily. "You don't find Evangeline's forest. You find a more realistic forest."

You find a huge white ash that has grown up at an angle of forty-five degrees and in a managed forest would have long ago been tagged for destruction. You find remarkably deep humus. You find a great rusty stump, maybe six feet high, and jagged where the trunk now beside it snapped off. More often, you find whole root structures tipped into the air and looking like radial engines. As you will nowhere else, you find the topography of pits and mounds. In its random lumpiness, it could be a model of glacial terrain. When a tree goes over and its roots come ripping from the ground, they bring with them a considerable mass of soil. When the tree has disappeared, the dirt remains as a mound, which turns Kelly green with moss. Beside it is the pit that the roots came from. When no other trace remains of the tree, you can see by the pit and the mound the direction in which the tree fell, and guess its approximate size. If cattle graze in pit-and-mound topography, they trample and destroy it. The pits and mounds of centuries are evidence of virgin forest.

There is supporting evidence in human records and in tree rings. People from Columbia University's Lamont-Doherty Earth Observatory have cored some trees in Hutcheson Forest and dated them, for example, to 1699, 1678. Neighboring land was settled, and cleared for farming, in 1701. Lamont-Doherty has an ongoing project called the Eastern Network Dendrochronology Series, which has sought and catalogued virgin stands at least two hundred and fifty years old. The list is short and scattered, and the tracts are small, with the notable exceptions of Joyce Kilmer Memorial Forest in North Carolina (thirty-eight hundred virgin acres), the cove hardwoods of Great Smoky Mountains National Park, and a large stand of hemlocks and beeches in Allegheny National Forest in western Pennsylvania. There are three hundred virgin acres on the Wabash River in Illinois, and, in eastern Ohio, a woods of white oak some of which were seedlings when the Pilgrims reached New England. The Ohio white oaks, like the white oaks of Hutcheson Forest, are from three to four feet in diameter. Old white oaks are found in few places, because they had a tendency to become bowsprits, barrel staves, and queen-post trusses. Virgin hemlocks are comparatively common. Maine is not rich in virgin timber—some red spruce on Mt. Katahdin, some red spruce above Tunk Lake. There is a river gorge in Connecticut where trees have never been cut. Some red spruce and hemlock in the Adirondacks date to the late fifteen-hundreds, and the hemlocks of the Allegheny forest are nearly two centuries older than that. In the Shawangunk Mountains, about seventy beeline miles northwest of mid-Manhattan, is the oldest known stand of pitch pine (360 years), also some white pine (370), chestnut oak (330), and eastern hemlock (500). They are up on a quartzite ridgeline, though, and are very slow-growing small trees. Remnant old-growth stands tend to be in mountains, in rocky, craggy places, not in flatlands. Hutcheson Forest, in the Newark Basin—in what was once a prime piedmont area—is thus exceptionally rare. In the region of New York City, there is nothing like it, no other clearly documented patch. In fact, it is the largest mixed-oak virgin forest left in the eastern United States.

Running through the forest is Spooky Brook, spawning ground of the white sucker. Rutgers would like to control the headwaters, fearing something known as herbicide drift. Continuing population drift is no less a threat, as development fills in lingering farms. The woods are closed to visitors, except for scheduled Sunday tours. Rutgers already owns some hundred and fifty acres contiguous to the forest, and hopes, with the help of the Nature Conservancy, to get two hundred more. Manipulative research is carried out on the peripheral land, while observational research goes on in the forest, which has been described by Richard Forman, a professor at Harvard, as "probably the single most-studied primeval woods on the continent." People have gone in there and emerged with more than a hundred advanced degrees, including thirty-six Ph.D.s. So many articles, papers, theses, and other research publications have come out of Hutcheson Forest that—as the old saw goes—countless trees have been clearcut elsewhere just in order to print them.

THE

GRAVEL

PAGE

■

"You have come from the Southwest, I see."

"Yes, from Horsham."

"That clay-and-chalk mixture which I see on your toe caps is quite distinctive."

"I have come for advice."

"That is easily got."

"And help."

"That is not always so easy."

"I have heard of you, Mr. Holmes."

For sixteen years, I have had on my desk petri dishes full of Platte River pebbles. They call to mind, among other things, kidnappings and murders—call to mind Sueyoshi Kusaba, Adolph Coors, the late Enrique Camarena. They call to mind Sherlock Holmes (as in the lines above, from "The Five Orange Pips"). They call to mind Karen Kleinspehn, Cecily Garnsey, Ronald Rawalt, James Swinehart. They call to mind Jimmy Doolittle, Joseph Corbett, Ken Lohman, Clarence Ross. And they call to mind always—as year follows year—the fact that I have not yet written this piece. The pebbles work these varied effects especially when they are wet. Worn, pitted, stream-rounded, they are without lustre when they are dry, but if you pour a little water on them, as I do from time to time to keep them alive, their colors brighten and shine. I took them from a gravel bar in Nebraska, near the river's right bank, not far from the hundredth meridian. From thirty-six thousand feet, as one passes over, the Platte there resembles a braid of cable. Its channels among the gravel bars are so numerous that the river is two miles wide. Choked with rock, the Platte cannot transport its load in any but an awkward way, so it subdivides and loops and braids, and hunts for passage through its own bed. From an altitude of thirty-six centimetres—we were lying prone, elbows down, chins in hand—the assembled gravel, like a New Hampshire boulder field, could be seen for what it was: unique sculpture from distinct terrane in widely separated distant worlds.

I was traversing the continent with Kleinspehn, a sedimentologist who was then a graduate student at Princeton University and is now a professor at the University of Minnesota. Choosing stones from the gravel bar, she was trying to guess where they might once have been bedrock. She picked up a stone of graphic granite—so called because its interlocking crystals develop in a manner that suggests writing. She said, "This is a real diagnostic pebble. If there's no graphic granite in the Laramie Range, it did not come from there." The Laramie Range, of the Wyoming Rockies, was only the most direct and obvious source of pebbles in a region of possibility at least the size of Italy, for the streams of the modern watershed were not the sole carriers; from numerous directions, there were ancient vanished rivers to be considered. In the core of the Laramie Range are the large slow-cooled crystals of a bright-pink granite called Sherman. Many of the pebbles beneath our eyes seemed surely to be Sherman granite, more than three hundred miles from where they had started. There were banded cherts and burgundy cherts. ("I have no idea where they came from; there are Mississippian cherts around the Black Hills.") There were gneisses, schists, and hard shales. There were foliated metamorphics, quartzites, quartz crystals ("from vein quartz in any rock—for example, from the Medicine Bow Mountains"). There were pebbles of red-bed sandstone. In the nineteen-thirties, a Nebraska man was indicted for stealing sheep from a ranch on Red Mountain, which is about twenty miles southwest of Laramie. Pleading not guilty, the defendant said that he had bought the sheep in Nebraska. In the sheep's wool were grains of red sandstone—Triassic red sand of the Chugwater formation, the rock of Red Mountain. Samuel H. Knight, of the Geology Department of the University of Wyoming, testified at the trial. There is Chugwater under Nebraska, yes, but it's hundreds of feet down.

I had read Raymond Murray and John Tedrow's textbook of forensic geology. Looking up contemplatively from the fast-moving Platte across a floodplain that ran off the curve of the earth, I realized that the concatenated pebbles Kleinspehn was describing not only were of varied provenance but also were, in macrocosm, directly analogous to the mineral assemblages that might be found, as dirt, on the skin or clothing of a hastily buried corpse. Detective work is what geologists do. In the long series of geological writings that I had undertaken, if I were to get into forensic geology this bar on the Platte River would be a place to begin.

I collected a sack of gravel and shipped it home. Over time, those prompting pebbles on my desk would send me off to unexpected places—to the Dakota Hogback in Jefferson County, Colorado, for example, and to the Pikes

Peak granite, farther south, and to the archives of the National Air and Space Museum, in Washington, and to the Materials Analysis Unit of the Federal Bureau of Investigation, also in Washington. The pebbles would draw me back to Nebraska—to the state geological survey, in Lincoln—and, by odd coincidence, to the river they came from, beside which lives a special agent who is an F.B.I. geologist.

At the state survey, I learned from the stratigrapher James Swinehart that Kleinspehn, despite the fact that she was only passing through, had been right at least nine times out of ten. In a sense, these pebbles were Swinehart's specialty. His expertise is in the Cenozoic paleogeography of western Nebraska. As I spilled before him what had been the contents of the dishes on my desk, he picked up the stones one by one, turned them in his hand, and occasionally looked closely at them under magnification. As he sorted them, he remarked that the line of maximum glacial advance lay east of my gravel bar, so there would be no agates from Minnesota, or greenstones, or the like—no evidence gathered from that direction. The sources would lie west and southwest, simplifying the situation by narrowing the field to a hundred thousand square miles. Taking two dark pebbles in the palm of his hand, he said they were acidic volcanics out of calderas in or beyond Rocky Mountain National Park—probably from the Rabbit Ears Pass area, near Steamboat Springs. To be geographically more specific, if you needed to be, you would have to analyze individual crystals under the microprobe, identifying major elements and trace elements.

Those Colorado calderas are four hundred airline miles from the river bar where I found the pebbles. How could he feel confident that that was where they came from? He had seen them before, he said—seen them uncounted times.

"I started out as an art-history major," he continued. "I learned the language. Someone asks you, 'How do you know that's a Vermeer?' It's like your grandmother walking down the street."

When Swinehart had finished sorting my collection, he was not surprised to see that the pink-feldspar Sherman granites were by far the largest group. In any attempt to pinpoint distant geographies, they would be less useful than, say, the Rabbit Ears volcanics. Sherman granite is the core not only of the Laramie Range but also of mountains in Colorado. Sources of granite, generally, are in "larger bodies and are therefore not as diagnostic."

Here, though, were a dozen pebbles of anorthosite—looking like blue cheese with their gray crystals and yellow weathery rinds—and one could say with certainty just where they came from. There is an anorthosite body of limited dimension in the Laramie Range northeast of Laramie. You would find a very large percentage of pebbles like these in Horse Creek coming out of the Laramies toward the Platte. A monomineralic rock, anorthosite is rare on this planet and very old. Unaccountably, it formed only during the Archean Eon and an era later in the Precambrian known as Neo-Helikian time. Westward, the next anorthosite outcrop would be in the San Gabriel Mountains, above Los Angeles. Eastward, there would be scattered outcroppings in the Canadian Shield. Anorthosite, in unearthly proportion, is the rock of all the high Adirondacks. Upward, it is plentiful in the night sky, being most of what you are looking at when you look at the moon.

Holding up a handful of sugary-textured fine-grained stones, some with green chlorite, Swinehart said, "These quartzites are almost surely from the Medicine Bow Mountains. They're very distinctive gravels, weathered out of a quartz-pebble conglomerate, in which the pebbles flattened.

The matrix has recrystallized, and so have the edges of the pebbles. The Medicine Bow quartzites and the anorthosite are so unusual in this geological situation that you can say just where they came from."

While a garden-variety granite might be hard to pin down geographically, if something in an assemblage is unusual the assemblage as a whole becomes useful. A banded ironstone from the Seminoe Range had travelled well over four hundred miles. It was two thousand million years old and it looked like petrified mahogany, a piece off the leg of a Steinway. "There's not a lot of it," he said. "But when it shows up it's a bull's-eye."

He did not know the name or home address of everything. He set aside a little pile that he referred to softly as "others."

"Others?"

"Ferrocryptomungite."

He had learned the term from an aeolian-sand expert in Denver, he said, and it meant, "It's ugly. You don't know what it is. And you hope it will go away." If you very much needed to know, you would make a thin section—a bit of rock ground to a thinness of three-hundredths of a millimetre and placed between microscope slides, from which its components, translucent, transparent, would flash their signature colors. If you were still unsure, you would do chemical analysis—"digest it and look at major ions." You could use X-ray diffraction and X-ray fluorescence spectroscopy or neutron activation to measure the elemental composition of the whole rock. To see a single crystal's chemistry, which might tie it to a source area, you would use a microprobe or inductively coupled plasma spectrometry. "You'd want to see at least a thin section before you'd publish it or take it to court," he went on. "Keep in mind —what questions are you really going to ask of these rocks?"

It may be comparatively simple to deal with a boulder, a cobble, a pebble, a granule, but when you fine down through grades of sand and reach the level of clay and silt, the degree of difficulty rises. "When you get below medium sand, you're off into chemistry-land. You'd better have a good reason for asking that question, because it's going to cost plenty to answer it. With separate feldspars, for example, you would need to look at the isotopic composition. That isn't cheap."

In choosing one pebble at a time and ascribing to it its place of origin, he was reversing a procedure more commonly applied to rock assemblages as a whole. I mean, if I had committed some unthinkable crime and run off to Florida and those pebbles had been found strewn about in my van Jim Swinehart or someone like him could have determined the provenance of each pebble in the group—and the distance of transport, and the presence and absence and percentages of rock types—and told anyone who needed to know that I had perpetrated whatever it was on a gravel bar in the main stem of the Platte River west of the line of glacial advance and east of the hundredth meridian. What works macroscopically works microscopically as well. Mineral grains and microfossils can narrate a story. A police officer fails to report for work in Harrisburg, Pennsylvania. His private automobile is found in Virginia, its trunk full of blood. The officer remains missing. Harrisburg police search the region for several days and come up with nothing. They turn for help to the F.B.I., which collects the officer's car and turns it over to Special Agent Ronald Rawalt, a geologist. With his petrographic microscope, not to mention his common sense, Rawalt studies the car. He sees a heavy buildup of soil in one wheel well and inside a bumper, and notes that the soil was wet-deposited. He sees also that the car was driven over pavement with water on it between the deposition time and the time the car was recovered. The soil is of one consistency, not the mottled layering from different locations that would usually be found under a fender. Someone stepped on the accelerator and spun the tire in mud. Like Rawalt, the Harrisburg police have assumed from the beginning that the soil in the wheel well is from a place where the body might be found. They just wonder where to look.

Going through the washed minerals, Rawalt finds microscopic fragments of glass beads and of yellow reflective paint and white reflective paint. The beads could be from any stretch of road, but the presence of both white and yellow paint suggests a hill or a curve. He finds microscopic asphalt. He finds black slag. He knows that Pennsylvania historically has bought slag from its iron smelters and coal-fired furnaces, crushing it for use as an anti-skid on highway curves. He also finds an assemblage of microfossils. He looks them up in a textbook of micropaleontology. The book includes maps. So unusual are these fossils that the pyritic limestone they come from outcrops only in two highly confined localities, one of them in Appalachian Pennsylvania. The limestone in Pennsylvania is just a narrow stringer that comes down off a mountain and crosses a country road south of Harrisburg. Rawalt calls the Harrisburg police. He mentions the road and tells them to stop at a rising curve where both yellow and white paint are present and there's not enough room for a whole car to get off the pavement. Since the missing man is heavy, look a short distance downslope. Next day, the police call Rawalt: "We got him. He was there, under a pile of brush."

■

"A sort of volcanic pit, was it not?"

"Exactly," said I.

"Did you notice the soil?"

"Rocks."

"But round the water—where the reeds were?"

"It was a bluish soil. It looked like clay."

"Exactly. A volcanic tube full of blue clay."

"What of that?" I asked.

"Oh, nothing, nothing," said he, and strolled back to where the voices of the contending men of science rose in a prolonged duet. [*"The Lost World"*]

F.B.I. geologists look first at color, and then at texture. Next they wash the soil and do the mineralogy. They collect "alibi samples," "alibi soils." If you have said that the mud on your skirt came from your back yard, they will collect soil from your yard to prove that it did or did not. About half the work of the Materials Analysis Unit has to do with geology. The rest has to do with things like glass and paint. Bruce Hall, the special agent who is the unit's chief in Washington, points out that forensic geology is broader than the name implies, because it includes chemistry and physics as well. It also includes, in growing numbers, people who testify about environmental impacts and the causal aspects of landslides. For my purposes here, the topic remains concentrated in military puzzles and egregious crimes.

Hall once spent a couple of days on Staten Island collecting alibi samples after a "soldier" in the Bonanno crime family put five dismembered bodies in several graves with a shovel. The shovel was found with bits of soil on its kick plate. Hall collected alibi samples from every place on Staten Island to which an alibi had been—or might be—ascribed. He matched the mineralogy from the bits of soil on the shovel to the mineralogy of the gravesites. With equal care, he unmatched everything else. "You've got to be right every time," he says. "There's no being wrong once in a while."

During the Cold War, the British traitor Kim Philby used a trowel to bury a hot camera in woods beside the Potomac River in Great Falls, Virginia. Years later, he evoked the scene in his autobiography, mentioning his fear of F.B.I. surveillance. After leaving the woods buttoning his fly, he went home and "fiddled around in the garden with the trowel." Apparently, he understood the potentialities of forensic geology, for he continued, "As far as inanimate objects were concerned, I was clean as a whistle."

Under Franklin, New Jersey, lies a sedimentary lead-zinc deposit that got caught up in metamorphism and crystallized some extremely weird minerals: black franklinite, green willemite, red zincite in white calcite. The assemblage is included as a taggant in some high explosives. If a marked explosive is used in a criminal way, it can be traced to its manufacturer and the store where it was bought.

If you were to find a trowel covered with galena, sphalerite, calcite, dolomite, and chalcopyrite in an easily discernible suite, you could say that it had been used somewhere near the Oklahoma-Kansas-Missouri intersection, a few miles west of Joplin.

Some years ago, I asked Chris Fiedler, an F.B.I. geologist, if he could think of a case in which the relevant rock had come in a size class larger than mud, silt, or sand. He remembered a time when the F.B.I. was investigating a group of potential terrorists thought to be moving explosives from safe house to safe house in eastern states. After a suspect vehicle passed through southern New Jersey, a large rock was observed near an intersection of roads. The F.B.I. wondered if the rock was a marker. They reasoned that the potential terrorists would assume that they were being followed and would use a lead car that was free of incriminating cargo. The lead car would set large rocks in predetermined places to inform a following car that things were so far so safe. Large rocks are about as common in South Jersey as bent grass on the swells of the ocean. South Jersey, above bedrock, is fifteen thousand vertical feet of unconsolidated marine sand. This rock was out of place, erratic, alien. The F.B.I. took it to Washington. It was a garnet schist, and in the schist was the mineral staurolite in a form sufficiently unusual to eliminate a lot of territory. A metamorphic petrologist at the Smithsonian Institution thin-sectioned the rock and determined that it came from a definable area in the highlands of western Connecticut. F.B.I. agents went there and began asking questions under the outcrops of garnet schist. They found the hideaway they were looking for. In it was evidence that ultimately led them to a safe house in Pennsylvania, full of explosives. The road had been circuitous, and that was the end of the line.

■

"It is evidently a case of extraordinary interest, and one which presented immense opportunities to the scientific expert. That gravel page upon which I might have read so much has been long ere this smudged by the rain and defaced by the clogs of curious peasants." [*"The Hound of the Baskervilles"*]

In Denver, years ago, Walter Osborne (an alias) bought a canary-yellow four-door Mercury sedan that had belonged to a couple whose name appears only as a black rectangle in F.B.I. files released under the law of freedom of information. The car was exceptionally clean. The old owners had washed it often, and they washed not just the paint and chrome surfaces, where dirt would show, but also the undercarriage, hosing everything from springs to wheel wells. Osborne was fastidious himself. He was an alkyd cooker at a Benjamin Moore paint factory, a job he did with highly commended care. He was on the night crew with one other person, had access to the factory offices, and—before he left—was able to remove every paper trace of his background.

Osborne had come to Denver to enrich himself through a single bold endeavor. Always thorough, he was not hurried. For several years, he made plans. Bank robbery had been his earlier choice, but after studying the field he came to the conclusion that there was not enough money in it. (He was closemouthed in general, but he did confide that much to a fellow-worker.) He decided instead that he could realize the kind of wealth he had in mind if he were to kidnap the chairman of a brewing company. His attention focussed on the patterns of custom at a modestly large house on Steele Street, in south Denver. He had all day, every day, to watch it. Adolph Coors III was the person he meant to abduct.

Osborne was who knows how close to choosing his moment when large vans appeared on Steele Street and the Coors family providentially moved. Privacy and insulation from any form of celebrity were what Ad Coors and his wife, Mary, wanted most for their four children—all teens or under. And so they had decided to try living on a fairly secluded ranch near Morrison, closer to the Rocky Mountain front, where they could go off on horseback when they wished to, on long anonymous rides. The change of milieu probably added about a year and a half to Ad Coors' life, but, inevitably, Osborne followed them.

The ranch was tucked into the morning shadow of the Dakota Hogback, a narrow, sinuous, phenomenal free-standing ridge that protrudes from the plains and parallels the mountain front for hundreds of miles. With its platy peaks, the ridge mimics the great mountains it borders. Cretaceous in age, it suggests not so much a modern razorback as the protruding spine of an unending stegosaurus. Dakota sandstone forms the high sharp parts, and these are underlain by gray, green, and maroon clay stones, shales, more sandstones, and limestone. A dirt road traversed the rising ground between the ranch and the ridge, and then crossed the ridge through a stream-cut gap. If you drove on that road—as Ad Coors did routinely on his way to work, as Osborne did in his yellow car—you were driving on the eroded, pulverized components of the Dakota Hogback.

Cecily Coors, at sixteen, often rode alone on the hogback, and often with her father. He was a tall man in his mid-forties with a wide grin and a quizzical nearsighted look behind his flesh-colored glasses. He was, in fact, so nearsighted that he would be—according to his ophthalmologist—lost without his glasses. In Cecily's irrepressible athleticism, her love of outdoor sport, she was much like him, and she raced him flat-out down trails in Aspen, flew with him in the company plane, went to Bears games with him in Denver. (One day, a good deal later than these scenes, she would be ranked third among downhill skiers in the United States.) There was a right-angle bend in the dirt road close to the hogback, and a wide flat space where a car could pull off. She passed by there on her way through the scattered junipers and up the sage-covered slopes. The yellow car was there, and there again. She would stop her horse and ask the driver if he wanted something. He thanked her, no. "He was always very friendly," she said recently, standing at the bend in the road. "We saw him a lot—up on our property. He had a very distinct face. He had, to me, a small face—with sunglasses. He always had a rifle with him."

They would have been prescription sunglasses, for Osborne was extremely nearsighted and could not have seen much of anything without them. She took him to be a hunter, a deer poacher, as her mother did on the several occasions when she, too, noticed the yellow car. Deer poachers scouting deer from automobiles were common in that country, never mind that it happened to be a game preserve. At least once when Cecily was riding with her father, they met Osborne at the bend.

Two miles from the ranch, on the east side of the hogback, was a wooden one-lane bridge over Turkey Creek. Almost every workday, Ad Coors crossed that bridge soon after eight in the morning—as Osborne had come to know. After Osborne decided that his planning was complete, he arrived at the bridge before eight one winter day, turned the yellow car around, backed up, and blocked the bridge on what would be, to the arriving Coors, the opposite side. Coors, listening to the radio in his International Travelall, left his ranch, went through the gap in the hogback, and turned north. Dressed, as he was, in a billed cap and a nylon windbreaker, not a suit, he would not have been taken for the chairman of a significant corporation on his way to his office. His tie, though, was secured by a clasp in the shape of a ski, and the ski was monogrammed "A C III." In his right rear pocket was a white handkerchief with maroon stitching: "A C III." On his key chain was a small silver penknife engraved "A C III." A label in his trousers said that Hickey-Freeman had "customized" them "expressly for Mr. A. Coors, III." His wristwatch was a Patek Philippe, Genève. He wore white deerskin gloves from Gokey. The tie—dark blue, with small white rings and red dots—was from the Aspen Country Store. The windbreaker was from Abercrombie & Fitch. He approached the bridge, got his two front wheels on it, and stopped in puzzlement, blocked by the yellow car. He seems to have rolled down his window and shouted something. He got out, closed the door, and faced Osborne—a heavy-shouldered man, with myopic eyes under a brown fedora. Neither man ever told this story, but evidence would carry the narrative. A woman whose house was several hundred yards away heard loud voices. If they were coming from the bridge, Ad Coors was resisting, re-acting to whatever Osborne might have said. The clash be-came physical. Both men's hats fell past the bridge railing and landed at the edge of the stream. Coors' eyeglasses came off his head and ended up in the water, a lens broken. Gun muzzle in Coors' back, Osborne seems to have tried to march him across the bridge toward the yellow car. Coors probably made a sudden move that electrified Osborne's nerves. The woman who had heard the shouting voices now heard gunfire. She would say it was the sound of lightning hitting a tree. Another woman—two and a half miles away, hanging laundry on an outdoor clothesline—heard it, too. Blood fell on the bridge railing and, in larger quantity, on the bridge. The yellow Mercury left the scene—digging out, leaving tracks, dirt flying.

Osborne's plans unravelled. In days that followed, he did not respond to responses to a typed ransom note that he sent to Mary Coors. His victim died. Burdened with a corpse, the yellow Mercury went south, outboard of the mountain front, and then, on an unpaved road in Douglas County, turned west and began to climb. There had been no snow in some time, and what there was had been scraped away. The road seemed to be made of mudded dust. Pink-feldspar dust. The dust was granite. If you were to collect such dust and do an analysis of it, it would look very much like granite. Compared with the source bedrock, the dust would be deficient in iron and magnesium, that's about all. The minerals break down at different rates. With altitude, the road became pebbly with granite, the hue brighter. It was old rock, ten times as old as the rock in the Dakota Hogback, but, as Colorado granites go, it was singularly and anomalously young. It was Pikes Peak granite—a geology that stands alone, and can write its name in dust. This was ponderosa country, its colors green and pink. At seven thousand two hundred feet, the yellow car turned in at a dump used by the Shamballah Ashrama, Brotherhood of the White Temple. Well beyond the mounded trash, the body was left in the forest. It would not be discovered—the fate of Ad Coors would not be learned—for seven months.

Returning to essentially clean pavement, Osborne now went east. Apparently, the next unpaved surface he drove on consisted of black slags and drifted sands on New Jersey's best-known barrier island. He all but hid the yellow car in some tall spartina grass near a large municipal dump. There, on the eighth day after the confrontation at the wooden bridge, he soaked the interior with gasoline and tossed in a lighted match. The fire was hot enough to melt some of the window glass. From the dump, it is only a fifteen- or twenty-minute walk to Mediterranean and Baltic, Park Place and the Boardwalk, and the rest of Atlantic City.

The F.B.I. gave a breathtaking performance in figuring out who Osborne was—assembling his story in dozens of ways, of which geological insight was just one. Something like thirty special agents worked on the case in Colorado, and a great many around the country. They learned that he was thirty-one—blue eyes, brown hair, a hundred and seventy pounds, six one, Caucasian. They learned that he had bought a .32 by mail order from Dakin Sporting Goods, in Bangor, Maine. They learned that he had practiced with his guns on targets at the Coors rifle range, near Golden. They learned that as a light and occasional drinker he preferred Coors. (They seem not to have learned that Ad Coors was allergic to beer.) They learned from their lab in Washington that the ransom note was probably written on a Royalite portable typewriter. A miner in the hogback, annoyed by frequent vandalism, said he tended to notice lingering cars, remembered a yellow Mercury, and was pretty sure that its license began with an AT and a 62. They attempted to do surveillance on each Mercury in Denver in the State of Colorado's 6200 series (colors were not listed), and they failed to locate only one. It was registered in the name of Walter Osborne, of 1435 Pearl Street, Denver. It had been bought from Hack Sells on the Little Lot, a dealer in Denver. A salesman confirmed the transaction and said the car was canary yellow. They learned that Osborne had worked at the paint factory. Although records were missing there, people remembered a number of things about him, including the fact that some five years back he had worked in Los Angeles for an ice company. The F.B.I. found the ice company, where Osborne had joined a union. Asked by the union to name a beneficiary for a life-insurance policy, Osborne had declined, saying that his parents were dead. Asked, then, to name a friend, he named Joseph Corbett, Sr., and gave an address in Seattle. Meanwhile, the lab in Washington matched a fingerprint on Osborne's first Colorado application for a driver's license to a fingerprint filed under fugitives from justice. It belonged to Joseph Corbett, Jr.

An F.B.I. agent in New Jersey, reading a description of Osborne's car, remembered the blistered hulk near the

Atlantic City dump. He checked its motor number. The F.B.I. in Colorado learned that Osborne could be an incautious driver. Two weeks before he ended the life of Ad Coors, he had been stopped by an officer of the Colorado State Patrol for crossing a yellow line and passing a truck at the crest of a hill. This was a few miles from the bridge that became the crime scene. When the policeman asked him what he thought he was doing, he answered flatly, "I got tired of waiting." After the F.B.I. learned that alias Osborne had paid his fine with a money order, they went to the National Check Cashing Company, which operated only in greater Denver, and went through four hundred thousand money orders. Of interest to them were five. They learned that he had ordered several sets of Monte Carlo handcuffs from Big Three Enterprises, on Sixth Avenue, in New York. Also cashed in New York was a money order that he had mailed to Kline's, on East Forty-second Street, a subsidiary of Prince Enterprises that handled only one product: leg irons.

They learned that ten days before the kidnapping-murder he was furiously writing to Blue Cross: "What is the meaning of this 'Final Notice of Payment Due'? I don't owe you one cent! . . . Billing people for goods and services they never ordered is a clear violation of the Fraud and Extortion section of the U.S. Postal Laws and regulations. I would suggest that you cease and desist before you find yourselves in serious trouble. Sincerely, Walter Osborne." He did not write that on the Royalite. He had long had another typewriter—a big standard Underwood 4—but he had written too much with it to trust it now, and clearly he bought the Royalite for the ransom note.

The F.B.I. went to May D & F, a Denver department store, whose label was in "The Cruiser"—the suspect's brown fedora. May D & F also sold Royalite portables, and, because typewriters have serial numbers, the store routinely recorded purchasers' names and addresses. Remarkably, a sales clerk remembered a cash sale that occurred four months before the crime. He looked through his files. The buyer was William Chiffins, of 1735 Pennsylvania Street, Denver. At the conclusion of the interview, the investigating agent showed the sales clerk five pictures. Did one of them resemble the buyer? That one, said the sales clerk, touching the likeness of Joseph Corbett, Jr.

Corbett had served in San Quentin and had later escaped from Chino. Second-degree murder. The F.B.I. knew that already. Reviewing the roster at San Quentin, they noticed that when Corbett was there Arthur John Cheffins was a prisoner, too. They learned from Cheffins that it had been his job to give I.Q. tests to fellow-prisoners. He remembered that Corbett had scored 148. It had also been Cheffins' job to give social-fitness tests. Corbett told Cheffins that he admired the intellect of Friedrich Nietzsche—especially the sentiment "Might makes right." If he said things like that, Cheffins advised Corbett, he could not give him much of a grade in social fitness. Corbett replied, "Look at Nagasaki. The only thing that was important was the result of the bomb."

Alias Osborne was seen at his apartment at five-thirty the morning after the scene at the bridge. In a locker in the basement he left a gasoline can, a two-burner Coleman gas stove, a nest of aluminum pots. In his apartment were two tent poles and a twelve-piece picnic set. All these things came from Sears. Figures had been added up on the carton that held the picnic set. A clerk at Sears remembered jotting down the figures, and remembered the buyer. He had come in after Christmas. He had inquired about a discount because the goods were out of season. The clerk asked why he wanted such equipment at that time of year. Corbett said, "I like to camp in winter. I'm going to camp this winter in the mountains."

Corbett was at large more than eight months. Meanwhile, the F.B.I. removed layers of material from under the fenders of the burned yellow Mercury and established the sequence of deposition. They collected four hundred and twenty-one "knowns"—Colorado earths of as many provenances—with which to compare "the questioned stuff." The analysis was assigned to Richard Flach, who, with a colleague nearly two decades earlier, had established forensic geology as a function of the F.B.I. Seven months after the crime, a pizza-truck driver who went target-shooting at the Shamballah Ashrama dump discovered the Hickey-Freeman trousers labelled "expressly for Mr. A. Coors, III." The engraved penknife was still in a pocket, and so was the maroon-monogrammed white handkerchief. The tie clasp and knotted tie and the Abercrombie & Fitch windbreaker—bullet holes in the back—were some distance away. Coors' wristwatch and gloves were separately found the next day. A few weeks later, the F.B.I. at last found Corbett: they pulled him out of a hotel in Vancouver, British Columbia, and walked him through the legal wickets that returned him to Colorado. When asked about the Coors kidnapping, he would fold his hands, lower his head, and resolutely say nothing about it. He was tried in Golden. He denied the presented story and never confessed. In the completed mosaic of evidence were enough solid items to condemn him many times over; the role of the geology was to tie him to the country.

While careful at all times to cover his tracks, he had been writing his itinerary on the bottom of his car. There were four depositional strata. The fourth and outermost contained the sands, silts, paper fibres, cinders, glass wools, and black slags that surround the Atlantic City dump. The sands of this fourth stratum were rounded and marine. All sand grains of the three inner layers were sharp and fresh. They contained the pink feldspars of the Pikes Peak granite, the pink feldspars of other Front Range granites, the light-gray quartzose sands of the hogback's Dakota Group, the varicolored sandstones, limes, and clays of the Morrison Formation. Richard Flach, now retired in Florida, refers to the oldest and innermost layer as "the odd man out, except that it could be related generally to the Rocky Mountain Front because of the pink feldspar." He goes on to say, "The second layer related to the country around Coors' ranch. It placed Corbett within a couple of miles of the crime scene. That is, it was consistent with the minerals of that locality, consistent with his being there. The third soil was from near where the body was found."

It was Flach's case—the testimony his to present. Flach was a geology-and-botany major from Northwestern University. The chief defense attorney was a graduate of the Colorado School of Mines. He attempted to discredit Flach, to impugn his competence. This led to a moment when an assistant defense attorney said, "I don't think he's qualified."

The judge said, "Sit down. He's qualified."

Corbett was sentenced to life imprisonment. The F.B.I. sent out a press release citing the "major importance" of the geologic evidence. Flach agrees softly: "It carried a little weight."

Corbett now lives free. Coors' daughter Cecily Garnsey lives with her husband in a community of town houses arranged for privacy but very close together, where small patches of lawn are decorated with little blue signs mentioning to intruders the prevailing security system. She accompanied me along the mountain front and up to the high ground of Shamballah Ashrama, where she had never been.

Under the ponderosas there, the big crystals of the Pikes Peak granite were crumbling like pink sugar. The air was warm, dry, at seventy-two hundred feet. She wore tennis shoes, tan shorts, a blue sleeveless canvas blouse, and pearl earrings. She was as trim as she had been on downhill skis. Shell casings of every calibre were all over the dump. Shoulder to shoulder, a score of special agents had walked here for days collecting her father's remains. She asked, almost of herself, "Didn't he bury him?" The dump was an ugly moment in beautiful terrain. After taking it in slowly, she described one of her sons, recently graduated from college, who had worked summers for the Arapahoe County police. "He's such a Sherlock Holmes person," she said. "He is waiting to get into the F.B.I."

■

For a long time he remained there, turning over the leaves and dried sticks, gathering up what seemed to me to be dust into an envelope, and examining with his lens not only the ground, but even the bark of the tree. ["The Boscombe Valley Mystery"]

Japan in 1944.

After a free-balloon flight test near the end of September, Technical Major Teiji Takada, of the Ninth Army Technical Research Laboratory, took a walk on the Ninety-nine League Beach, at Ichinomiya. Satisfied with the test, of which he was in charge, he simultaneously rejoiced in the temporary relief from pressures applied by his military superiors and began to concentrate on another question. "The only thing left for further study was the planning of how to meet the requirement of huge amount of sand on the beach," he later wrote. (The translation, done six years after the war, is by Ken Suda, of the Central Meteorological Observatory, in Tokyo.) "After the balloon has disappeared in the blue sky, I walked about on the sand beach, picked up a handful of sand at several places to wrap it in a piece of paper and putting it in my pocket, went down the sand dune in the evening dark feeling the chill of autumn wind."

It had been a long two and a half years since B-25s from the American carrier Hornet, under the command of Lieutenant Colonel James Doolittle, bombed Kobe, Nagoya, Yokosuka, Yokohama, and Tokyo, agitating the Japanese populace, embarrassing the military, and setting in motion the free-balloon project that was now about ready. It was intended specifically as retaliation for the Doolittle raid. The unmanned balloons were meant to carry fire bombs and high-explosive bombs to the homeland of the United States and drop them there to kill people, destroy structures, and start forest fires. The preparation had consumed so much time because the technological problems were acute. This was not a simple matter of loading up some bottled germs and floating them over Russians in Manchuria, as the Japanese had once done. These balloons had to travel more than five thousand miles. In sunlight they would rise and in darkness fall. With excessive rising and falling, they would fail their mission. They would also fail their mission if they leaked too much hydrogen. They should not drop their bombs until they reached North America. Bombs away, the balloons should then destroy themselves.

In addressing and fulfilling each requirement, Technical Major Takada and his numerous colleagues at the research laboratory and their boss—Major General Sueyoshi Kusaba—were creating an intended instrument of terror, the world's first intercontinental ballistic missile, a

Japanese V-1 with twenty times the range, if not the accuracy, of the German rocket. The jet stream was not yet called by that name, but the great strong current of the winter air—in its sinuosity and remarkable velocity—had been the recent discovery of the Japanese, and the jet stream, they calculated, could drive a large balloon to North America in three days. You could find the high wind at and above thirty thousand feet. With an altimeter and a battery, you could cause gunpowder to ignite and jettison ballast when a balloon, cruising, descended to thirty thousand feet. They tested that successfully. With an altimeter and a valve, you could get rid of hydrogen if the sun were to expand it to a critical extent. You could program the valve to release hydrogen at thirty-eight thousand feet. That, also, they tested successfully. Within these designated altitudes, in the jet stream, a balloon would go through x cycles in y hours, expending z pounds of ballast. Now the balloon is over the United States. The ballast is gone. The next discharge of gunpowder releases the bombs and lights a sixty-four-foot fuse that dangles like a shroud line from the balloon's equator. For eighty-two minutes, the fuse shortens, and then it ignites a flash bomb that blows up the envelope. Mission accomplished, missile destroyed. To carry all that gear, the balloon would need a lifting capacity, at sea level, of one thousand pounds. You could do that with a diameter of ten metres.

At first, the balloons were made of conventional rubberized silk, but there was a way to make an envelope that would leak even less. An order went in for ten thousand balloons made of *washi*. Produced in rectangular units not much larger than a road map, *washi* was paper, derived from a mulberry that was much like American sumac. Practically impermeable and very tough, it represented a step backward to a higher technology, like a bark canoe. In three or four laminations, the paper was glued with devil's-tongue flour. Devil's-tongue is a Japanese potato. Workers stole the paste and ate it. Many workers were high-school girls, whose fingers were nimbler than the fingers of any other class of people. They were told to wear gloves, to keep their fingernails short, and not to use hairpins. They assembled the paper in many parts of Japan. They had no idea of the purpose of their work. When scuttlebutt suggested the truth to them—that they were making *fusen bakudan* that would fly all the way to America and ignite fires—they laughed. Large indoor spaces were required for the envelope assembly—sumo halls, soundstages, theatres—but somehow secrecy was preserved.

Before preparations were complete, B-29s attacked the home islands, and the balloon project that had begun as an act of revenge became an act of desperation. At last, the balloons were ready. The jet stream was ready. The order came down to release at 0500 on November 3rd. Ichinomiya, on the Chiba Peninsula, east-southeast of Tokyo, was one of three launching sites. Major Takada watched as the products of ten years' research and two years' labor were let go, one by one. In his words, "The figure of the balloon was visible only for several minutes following its release until it faded away as a spot in the blue sky like a daytime star."

The Military Geology Unit of the United States Geological Survey was established in June of 1942, six months after the Japanese attack on Hawaii and virtually at the same time that work was beginning in Japan on the intercontinental balloons. The Geological Survey people had imagined that geological knowledge could help the military effort, so they made up a sample folio of information useful to an invading army, randomly choosing Sierra Leone as a model. They located water supplies, strategic minerals, and places where road-building materials could be obtained. They described the terrain. According to Kenneth Lohman, who was one of the original geologists in the section, "The War Department bought it hook, line, and sinker," but the utility of such folios would be greatly reduced by a distinct and unexpected problem: "The military, we found out, couldn't read a topographic map." Presented with contours, depressions, noses, and reëntrants on a flat sheet of paper, the military people tended not to see terrain in three dimensions. Therefore, as the geologists began making folders on strategic settings all over the world, they developed terrain diagrams—pen-and-ink sketches of landscape as if from a low-flying plane.

Ken Lohman is ninety-eight years old. I met him when he was ninety, and interviewed him in, among other places, a hospital room in Virginia, before I had to suppress my interest in forensic geology in order to spend a number of years on the geology of California. When I next telephoned Lohman, to inquire about renewing our talks, he was ninety-seven. He said—a little more than firmly, and with emphasis on the first and third words—"Where have you been?"

I went to see him at his home, in Fairfax Station, Virginia, near Washington. A few years ago, he stopped going regularly to his office at the Survey. I found him, as before, engaging, direct, humorous, and amiable. He speaks in a strong low-register voice. He is tall and large-framed, and his hair is now for the most part fringe, superthin on top. He is out of the habit of a bourbon-and-water every night before dinner, a Martini at the Cosmos Club before lunch on Fridays. He has thick eyeglasses. He peers at you from behind the glass like a teller from a cage.

"We worked eighteen hours a day," he reminded me, speaking of the war years. "We practically slept on the job.

We helped the military pick landing beaches. We were look-ing for places with shallow water near shore, not a shelving beach or a cliffy shore. No quicksand." They worked in the Interior Building, only two physical blocks but two thousand political miles from the White House, for the Geological Survey at that time had a long way to go to please, if not placate, the sitting President. As geologists of the day would tell you, Roosevelt didn't like the Survey. First, Herbert Hoover was a geologist, a mining engineer. Second, Roo-sevelt had a special interest in the properties of the water at Warm Springs, Georgia, which he had found therapeutic for the polio that had stricken him in 1921, and as early as 1927 he had written a request to the Survey for a study of the Warm Springs water, seeking an analysis of its ob-viously distinguished chemistry. The Survey replied that you could find similar water in the pipes of an average city. In a consequent exchange of letters, Roosevelt expressed con-siderable annoyance. When he became President, his re-quest for a thorough study acquired mass. Foster Hewett, of the United States Geological Survey, was named leader of a team that went to Georgia. There—to Hewett's surprise—he encountered a German consultant. This was Doktor Paul Haertl, managing director of Bad Kissingen, consultant also to Saratoga Springs. Even while Hewett was making the scene, Roosevelt was seeking a second opinion.

The American and the German conferred. At one point, Doktor Haertl asked Hewett, "Are you studying the gas that comes from the water?"

Hewett answered, "We are."

Haertl said, "Have you examined the shape of the bubbles?"

Hewett's pupils doubled in size. He said, "No, we haven't."

Haertl said, "Oh, you must examine the bubbles. Some bubbles are round, but others are square."

Hewett (all this would appear in U.S. Geological Survey Bulletin 1589) said, "Do I understand that you know places in Germany where the bubbles issuing from water are square?"

"Oh, yes, Mr. Hewett," Haertl said. "The bubbles of gas at Bad Kissingen are square. You see, Mr. Hewett, when you put your arm in water that contains gas, bubbles appear on the flesh. Now, if these bubbles are round they produce no effect, but if they are square they have the effect of stimulating the nerves of the skin. It is extremely important that you determine whether these bubbles are round or square."

Hewett spent two and a half years studying Warm Springs, and concluded that the magic fluids were "ordinary rain water without exceptional physical or chemical properties." It fell on Pine Mountain, followed a bed of quartzite to a depth sufficient to heat it, and came up along a fault. After this information was printed in his report, a bound copy was sent to the White House. It was not acknowledged.

Ken Lohman commented, "There was a period of about six years in the thirties when no one was hired by the Survey. Roosevelt wanted to believe the German, who said the bubbles came up in the water and the corners scratched your skin. That was just bullshit."

When the Survey's Military Geology Unit began its work, it consisted of Lohman and five others in a very small corner of the Interior Building's fifth floor. "In no time, it was two hundred, and we had the whole floor," Lohman said. These geologists all had broader backgrounds in the science than geologists would tend to have in later years— a fact that fit the spread of war. By year-end 1944, they had contributed several hundred major studies across the whole spectrum from invasions to defenses, reconstituting, at the

White House, the Survey's lost prestige. Their principal link with the military was Colonel Sidman Poole, G-2—"a fine man," as Lohman remembers him, "a bit on the pompous side, as colonels usually were." One day early in the New Year, "Poole came in with a couple of little bags of sand. Very much hush-hush. People who weren't classified couldn't even get into the place. Poole wanted to know where the damned sand came from."

Balloons had been sighted, explosions heard, from California to Alaska. Something that appeared to witnesses to be like a parachute descended near Thermopolis, Wyoming; a fragmentation bomb exploded in bright-red flame; shrapnel was found around the crater. Actually, the paper balloons were shaped much like our hot-air balloons that float in the morning and evening sky, and were about three-quarters as large. As is detailed in Robert C. Mikesh's "Japan's World War II Balloon Bomb Attacks on North America," a P-38 Lockheed Lightning brought down a paper balloon near Santa Rosa, California, another was seen over Santa Monica, and bits of *washi* paper were found in the streets of Los Angeles. Two paper balloons were recovered in a single day in Modoc National Forest, east of Mt. Shasta. Near Medford, Oregon, a balloon bomb exploded in thirty-foot flames. The Navy found balloons in the ocean. A P-47 Thunderbolt brought one down in the Aleutians. Balloon envelopes and other apparatus were found near Kalispell, Montana; Lame Deer, Montana; Nogales, Arizona; Estacada, Oregon; Stony Rapids, Saskatchewan. Balloons came down at Fort Simpson, on the Mackenzie River, in the Northwest Territories; and at Marshall and Holy Cross, Alaska, in the Yukon-Kuskokwim delta—failing, like so many others, to destroy themselves.

Under the headline "BALLOON MYSTERY," *Newsweek* of January 1, 1945, told a story about two woodchoppers who found the balloon at Kalispell. On January 2nd, an item appeared in the New York *Times* under the headline

BALLOON IN OREGON
Like That Found in Montana
It Is Laid to Enemy Origin

The Office of Censorship sent out an all-points memorandum to newspapers and radio stations asking them to make no mention of balloons and balloon-bomb incidents, lest the enemy be encouraged to release even more.

Where conventional balloons would have a hanging basket, the *fusen bakudan* had a cast-aluminum four-spoke wheel festooned with sandbags, like bulbs pendant from a chandelier. The sand device developed by Technical Major Takada was an automated hopper. For the most part, though, the sand was precisely weighed in amounts of as little as three and as much as seven pounds, and wrapped in paper identical to the paper of the envelope, snugly secured with twine. These ballast units were programmed in pairs for sequential release by the battery-and-altimeter gunpowder method, always getting rid of two bags at once, on opposite sides of the ring, so as not to tilt the envelope and risk losing gas. Most of the ballast was gone by the time a balloon crashed in North America, but a few sandbags were found. And the War Department asked Colonel Poole if his geologists could tell where the sand came from.

Remember, it was inconceivable that the balloons had travelled five thousand miles from Japan. American Military Intelligence was no more prepared to believe that than were the high-school girls who were gluing the paper in numerous parts of Honshu. It was thought that the balloons must be coming from North American beaches, launched by landing parties from submarines. It was thought that the balloons might also, or alternatively, be coming from the submarines themselves. It was thought that the balloons might be coming from German prisoner-of-war camps, or from Japanese-American relocation centers. They might even be coming from small Pacific islands. Possibly their purpose was to transport enemy agents. Poole handed over to the geologists several cupfuls of sand.

One close look and they eliminated North America. Everything was wrong. It was not our sand. Chemically, petrologically, it was not the sand of the mid-Pacific, either. The geologists, with their polarizing microscopes and their dark-field stereoscopic microscopes, settled in for a tighter view. Ken Lohman was more or less in charge. He is a micropaleontologist and a specialist in diatoms, a class of microscopic algae. He was not discouraged by the palmful of sand that was given to him. "It was enough to work on, anyway. I stewed up the stuff, and I got more than a hundred species of diatoms." The sand had obviously come from a beach. It contained a mixture of recent diatoms and fossil diatoms, and that, to Lohman, meant beach sand. The geologists read the papers of Hisashi Kuno on orthopyroxenes from volcanic rocks, which dated only to 1937 but had quickly established him as one of the world's most gifted petrologists. His paper on Hakone Volcano was the most detailed study ever made of that kind of rock. Reading Kuno in the light of the mineral percentages they were seeing in the sand, they eliminated chunks of country.

Julia Gardner was a paleontologist whose most concentrated experience was in small mollusks. She put the ballast under her microscope and looked at pieces of small mollusks. She looked as well for coral. You can identify coral even if it is smaller than a sugar grain. There was no coral—not a hint of coral. Coral doesn't grow in cold water. Along the coasts of Japan, the northern boundary of coral comes near the latitude of Tokyo. It approximates the thirty-fifth parallel. Gardner was eliminating the southern third of Japan.

Clarence Ross—mineralogist, petrologist—found nothing granitic in the mineral assembly. His son Mac Ross, himself a Survey mineralogist, recently remarked to me, "If the sand had derived from a garden-variety granite, it would have been difficult to trace, or impossible, but it contained an unusual suite of minerals." His father and the others looked at geologic maps of Japan, and eliminated all beaches north of the thirty-fifth parallel where streams reached inland to granite bedrock. That done, the search became more subtle. The assemblage included hypersthene, augite, hornblende, garnet, high-titanium magnetite, high-temperature quartz. Most remarkably, the hypersthene was fifty-two per cent of the total. Even allowing for wave concentration of this heavy mineral, so large a percentage was quite unusual. The hypersthene and the augite would be of volcanic origin. Augite is typical in volcanic rocks, hypersthene a good deal less so. The hornblende and the garnet were metamorphic, so you'd have to see both volcanic and metamorphic rocks upstream from the beach. The high-titanium magnetite was igneous in origin. In Mac Ross's words, "The assemblage does look a bit strange. The high-temperature quartz suggests melts that you would expect from lava flows. You wouldn't find that in Hawaiian basalts. Shards of glass in the sands also speak of lavas. There's no mica. As euhedral crystals, hypersthene grows in a melt. The crystals are then erupted. They are frozen into a volcanic glass. What follows is the weathering out of the glass. How it got to be fifty per cent is strange. There's so much hypersthene that you'd have to have a local igneous rock that was not all that common."

Patiently, exhaustively, Clarence Ross searched the literature, studied the maps, and related the rock types to his own petrologic descriptions. He was a large, imposing man with a mane of gray hair. His son says of him, "He had a professorial manner. There was no trivia. Small talk was beyond him. He was forty-nine when I was born, so in some ways he was like a grandfather. When he came home, he always smelled of immersion oils." Mac's wife, Daphne, remembers her father-in-law as "a forthright person with a dominant personality, a perfectionist, who didn't take fools lightly." Ken Lohman describes him as "an oddball guy, not sociable, a damned good man on rocks, without much interest in anything else," and says, "His stuff was definitive."

Kathryn Lohman, who had been a specialist in foraminifera for Texaco, looked through the ballast sands for these single-celled microscopic creatures with calcareous shells. Forams are highly varied, fairly ubiquitous, almost wholly marine, and have been around more than five hundred million years. Kathryn found quite a few of them that had been described north of Tokyo and on the east coast of Japan. On this planet, they occurred nowhere else. "She went to the Smithsonian and got papers from Japan," Ken Lohman told me. "Her forams were just as definitive as the diatoms were." When I asked him to describe her, he said, "Anything I say would be colored by the fact that I was very much in love with her. She was very good-looking. She played the piano beautifully. I played the violin. We never had a harsh word in fifty years. It was easy to like her. She was friendly."

Kathryn was born in Canada, grew up in Winnipeg. I had asked the question in their living room, she gone now thirteen years, he aged ninety-seven. As I looked around the room, I saw fresh newspapers, copies of *Physics Today*, copies of *Science News*. A headline on a geological publication said, "Gulf's Mahogany Find Excites Explorers." There was a church-model Hammond organ and eleven speakers—five for the Hammond, six for the stereo. Spread out on a table were his Beethoven sonatas, his Beethoven concertos, his Haydn symphonies, his copy of Jules Verne's "A Journey to the Center of the Earth." Outside were his hundreds of azaleas. He remarked out of nowhere that he was expecting momentarily a load of mulch.

I concentrate here on Ken Lohman because he is an eminent, arresting scientist, and because he is alive. "In 1993, I developed an irregular heartbeat," he said, evidently reading my mind. "It was very scary. You could die from it. But I'll never go to another nursing home. God Almighty."

Here and there on the walls were pictures in rich color—a third of a metre wide—of intricately patterned circular objects that came close to resembling Buddha's gongs. They were diatoms, magnified seven thousand three hundred times. In my notes somewhere was the first description he gave me of these creatures on which he had centered his life's work: "They're just damned interesting things to look at. They're beautiful. They're useful fossils, Cretaceous to Recent. Hydrosilica, $SiO_2 \cdot nH_2O$—the same composition as opal. There are no opals before the Cretaceous, and no diatoms before the Cretaceous. There's no connection, but it's interesting. The average size of a diatom is forty to sixty microns. A big diatom is two hundred microns."

A micron is a thousandth of a millimetre. I remarked that a Princeton professor of geology had told me that all the diatom experts in the history of the world have yet to look through their first teaspoonful of diatoms.

Lohman said, "That is wrong. It's more like a table-spoonful."

Following my gaze to the pictures on the wall, he said, "They have very fine structures—beautiful structures, and very reliable. Identification can be done without doubt. They have rows of little dots, for example, so many microns apart. With some diatoms, thirty-seven thousand dots would make an inch. Whatever the spacing, the spacing is uniform for a species. They always live in water, even in moist soil. They have to live in sunlight. They are generally thought to be plants, but they move around; they store food. They're one-celled. They have a peculiar scattery locomotion. They don't know where they're going, like a lot of people. They inhale carbon dioxide and they expel oxygen, which must propel them."

There are three hundred genera of diatoms and twenty-five thousand species. "I've had seventy-five years of looking at these buggers. You get to recognize them. You know two or three thousand species just like that. You can take a look at a slide and say, 'That's Middle Miocene.' Lake-surface diatoms are totally different from bottom ones. Diatoms live on ice floes. They live in hot springs. There are twenty-one million diatoms per cubic inch of diatomite. In one litre of seawater are a hundred thousand to one million diatoms. The water is clear—it doesn't even look cloudy, they're so small."

Lohman dropped out of Caltech after his freshman year. He learned photography. Johns Manville hired him to photograph diatoms for advertising purposes. Johns Manville mined diatoms. ("All the sugar you have ever eaten has been filtered through diatoms.") He also found a job as a chemist. His chemistry was from Hollywood High School and the freshman year at Caltech.

One day, his boss said to him, "Do you have a Ph.D. from Harvard?"

Lohman said, "I don't have a Ph.D. from anywhere. I don't have an undergraduate degree."

The boss looked oddly pleased.

Lohman asked him why he had said "a Ph.D. from Harvard."

The boss said, "Your predecessor had a Ph.D. from Harvard and he wasn't worth a fart in a high wind."

Lohman eventually went back to Caltech—a freshman in 1916, a sophomore in 1926. He completed his undergraduate degree and did graduate work there to the master's level. When he was working in the Military Geology Unit during the war, he did not yet have a Ph.D. In the nineteen-fifties, on leave from the Geological Survey, he would return to Caltech to complete it.

As the research went forward on the fifth floor of the Interior Building, balloons continued to arrive in North America. Near Klamath Falls, Oregon, a snowplow plowed into one. Balloons came down in or dropped their bombs on Bigelow, Kansas; Holstein, Iowa (incendiary explosion); Nelson House, Manitoba; Oxford House, Manitoba; Waterhen Lake, Manitoba; Fort Chipewyan, Alberta (in all, four balloons landed around Lake Athabasca); Hay River, Northwest Territories (bits of envelope, two unexploded incendiaries, seven sandbags beside the Great Slave Lake); the Brooks Range (two); Echo, Oregon (now in the National Air and Space Museum); Walla Walla, Washington; American Falls, Idaho (bomb burst in air, fragments were found); Kadoka, South Dakota; Pyramid Lake, Nevada; Delta, Colorado (explosion, shrapnel); Desdemona, Texas; Laguna Salada, Mexico; Grand Rapids, Michigan; and—the longest known flight, ending in a shower of incendiary fragments —Farmington, Michigan, ten miles from the center of Detroit.

"I should have got a Purple Heart," Ken Lohman told

me. "I was working so hard I got hemorrhoids. They'd find another balloon. Poole would come in with another handful of sand."

The fossil diatoms—their number and variety notwithstanding—were all Pliocene in age, and that removed from consideration a great deal of parent rock. In an 1889 paper by the French paleontologists Jacques Brun and Joannes Tempere, Lohman found descriptions of diatoms identical to the ones in the ballast sands. The research area of the Brun and Tempere paper was around Sendai, on the Honshu coast northeast of Tokyo. He also read papers by "Japanese diatomaniacs," who described the same fossils on the same coastline. Brun and Tempere covered forams, too, and they were the forams that Kathryn Lohman was finding in the ballast sand. Taking these things together with the discoveries of Clarence Ross and Julia Gardner, the Military Geology Unit, which had already narrowed its focus to the northerly thousand miles of Japan's eastern coasts, now narrowed that by eighty per cent. More scientific literature, more sand, more study of geologic maps, and they were ready to be specific. They told Colonel Poole that the sands seemed to have come from one or both of two locations, roughly two hundred miles from each other. Only because of the coral line, the geologists slightly favored the more northerly site—the great beach of Shiogama, close to Sendai. To the other site the minerals were even more closely matched, but the coral line was so near that if it was the launching place of the sand under their microscopes they would expect to see a trace amount of drift coral, and none was there. The southerly site was the Ninety-nine League Beach at Ichinomiya.

Joseph Conrad's Charlie Marlow, sailing down the coast of Africa on his way to the heart of darkness, passed a French man-of-war anchored near "the edge of a colossal jungle so dark-green as to be almost black, fringed with white surf." The French ship was firing its guns. "There wasn't even a shed there, and she was shelling the bush. . . . In the empty immensity of earth, sky, and water, there she was, incomprehensible, firing into a continent." Only in the postwar's lengthening hindsight did Japan's balloon campaign reach the metaphorical status of that French warship. General Kusaba launched more than nine thousand bomb-laden paper balloons. It was his hope and expectation that ten per cent would complete the flight to North America. Physical evidence of some three hundred of them was found on the North American mainland. A reasonable estimate is that a thousand made the crossing. Only two landed in Japan—one on northern Honshu, one on Hokkaido. No damage. In the end, the balloons represented the enemy's fourth and last and most sustained attack on the United States mainland in three years and eight months of war. In February of 1942, Japanese Submarine I-17 shelled an oil field up the beach from Santa Barbara, and damaged a pump house. In June, Submarine I-25 shelled a coastal fort in Oregon, damaging a baseball backstop. In September of 1942, the I-25's crew assembled and launched a Yokosuka E-14Y-1—a small float plane—that attacked Oregon. Its incendiary bombs ignited small fires on a ridge of Mt. Emily. The balloon campaign killed six Americans, all in an instant. Five of them were Sunday-school children. A minister and his wife took them on a fishing trip in southern Oregon, east of the Cascades. The minister was some distance away when his wife and the children came upon a balloon bomb. They called to him in excitement, and a moment later were dead.

All through that fall and winter, airplanes scrambled in pursuit of the balloons, but the airplanes were singularly unsuccessful. Lightnings, Hellcats, Thunderbolts, Corsairs, they literally were not up to it, and they destroyed fewer than twenty, only two of them over the United States. In altitude and sometimes in speed, the paper balloons were beyond the reach of American interceptors. On the coast of Washington, the Fourth Air Force set up a balloon early-warning line—Cape Flattery to Queets to the mouth of the Columbia River. One result of a secret meeting of military planners on January 17, 1945, was this classified statement: "Should balloons approach in hours of darkness, visual observation will not be effective." Frequently, pilots reported balloon sightings and the balloons turned out to be Venus.

Japanese propaganda broadcasts mentioned great fires and an American populace in panic. One broadcast said that five hundred casualties had occurred. Another broadcast raised the figure to ten thousand. Several million airborne Japanese troops were said to be ready to follow the balloons. The woman and five children who died in Oregon were the only American mainland casualties of the Second World War.

Geologists would develop some hyperbole of their own, especially after the war, when stories about the accomplishments on the fifth floor of Interior enriched the scientific conversation. Of the three balloon-launching sites, Ichinomiya was nearest to Tokyo. The two others—Nakoso and Otsu—were scarcely ten miles apart and about a hundred miles up the coast from Ichinomiya, in the direction of Shiogama, the survey's other suggested beach. So far so true. Not without encouragement from Colonel Poole, the geologists tended to make a memorable story even more memorable. After the Survey's sand analysis, according to Ken Lohman, "Jimmy Doolittle went over and bombed hell out of the place." He said Poole told them that in so many words. He said, "We had all kinds of classified information.

It wasn't in the newspapers, don't worry. Doolittle came up from Okinawa and bombed hell out of the whole area. The Japanese general was crestfallen." From geologists over the years, I've heard many versions of the same remark: "Photoreconnaissance showed the plant. Jimmy Doolittle bombed the bejeezus out of it, and there weren't any more balloons."

B-29s destroyed two of the three hydrogen plants that supplied the balloon project. Jimmy Doolittle was there in spirit. General Kusaba was indeed disappointed—a sentiment he expressed in person to a visitor from the United States Geological Survey late in 1945. By April of that year, Kusaba had spent nine million yen on his balloon campaign. In the military structure were people higher than Kusaba who considered that a very great waste of yen. He was ordered to give up the launchings. "Many factories which were manufacturing various parts of balloons were destroyed," he later told a reporter. "Moreover, we were not informed about the effect of this weapon throughout the wartime. Due to the mentioned hardships, we were compelled to cease operations." The American press, in its way, had been as effective as the B-29s, for what Kusaba needed in order to impress his superiors and keep his project going was proof that the people of the United States, in dread of the balloon missiles, were in psychological disarray. From the American press Kusaba had nothing to show. After the deaths of the children in Oregon, the War and Navy Departments in Washington at last broke the silence of censorship with press releases informing the public of the danger. Headlines quickly bloomed, some in full eight-column width: "JAP BALLOONS REACH COAST" (San Francisco *Chronicle*), "NIP BALLOONS HAVE LIT IN WEST, ARMY REVEALS" (San Francisco *Call-Bulletin*). Soon Smilin' Jack—comic-strip aviator, lantern-jawed Lindbergh

—was encountering paper balloons. But they were just newspaper balloons. The real ones had stopped coming.

The coast around Otsu and Nakoso, backed with granite highlands, had been considered unlikely by the Survey as a site for launchings. To Lohman and his colleagues, being right on one site and missing the two others was a matter of zero discomfort. "We always got the same kind of sand," he told me. "The samples we had were all from the same beach."

In a magazine article in 1953 Lincoln LaPaz wrote, "Scientists studying the balloons in this country (I was one of them) believed that the next step on the Japanese war plan, scheduled for the fall of 1945, was to be a balloon-borne bacteriological attack." A university cosmologist, LaPaz during the war had been technical director of the Second Air Force Operations Analysis Section. About the atomic bombs exploded over Hiroshima and Nagasaki, he wrote, "Some people talked about how inhuman we Americans were. If they had only known what we avoided! I don't know how much influence the anticipated Japanese balloon offensive had on President Truman's decision to use the bomb, but it seems reasonable to guess it was a factor in his consideration."

On March 10, 1945, a paper balloon that had crossed the Pacific Ocean, the Olympic Mountains, and the Cascade Range descended in the vicinity of the Manhattan Project's production site at Hanford, Washington. The balloon landed on an electric line that fed power to the building containing the reactor that was producing the Nagasaki plutonium, and shut the reactor down.

■

"Well, Watson, I will not offend your intelligence by explaining what is obvious. The gravel upon the window sill was, of course, the starting-point of my research. It was unlike anything in the vicarage garden. Only when my attention had been drawn to Dr. Sterndale and his cottage did I find its counterpart." ["The Adventure of the Devil's Foot"]

When the textbook "Forensic Geology," by Raymond C. Murray and John C. F. Tedrow, appeared, in 1975, its jacket copy lavished credit on Sherlock Holmes as the progenitor of this branch of the science. The text within was more restrained, and ascribed the credit to Conan Doyle. It quoted Dr. Watson on Holmes' knowledge of geology: "Practical, but limited. Tells at a glance different soils from each other. After walks has shown me splashes upon his trousers, and told me by their colour and consistence in what part of London he had received them." But the textbook's authors—professors of earth sciences at Rutgers University—were too serious to lean on the wisdom of the detective himself, and did not quote him. If they had, they might have increased—even more than they did—the number of geologists in the F.B.I., all of whom have the book. For the most part, they are F.B.I. geologists as a result of reading it. Chris Fiedler, for example, who started out doing clerical work for the Bureau, happened to have geological training. After he came upon Murray and Tedrow's textbook, he had himself transferred to the lab.

The Geological Survey and the Smithsonian stand ready to help. The F.B.I. prefers the Smithsonian. Not only is it just across Constitution Avenue but it is also generous in donating its time and effort, whereas the Geological Survey might present a stiff bill. Once a suite of minerals has been washed and sorted out, it can readily be presented to people like Daphne Ross for powder X-ray diffraction,

Eugene Jarosewich for the electron microprobe, Sorena Sorensen and Victoria Avery for cathodoluminescence. A cathode-ray tube shoots electrons into a sample, and, in Sorensen's words, "images the presence of trace elements." She remarks on her astonishment at the role mineralogy can play: "You can fingerprint soil samples from a crime scene. You see how special two rocks a hundred metres apart can be."

For some F.B.I. geologists, Constitution Avenue could not be called convenient. Ron Rawalt lives on the South Platte River, in North Platte, Nebraska, where he and his wife have three children and ten acres. "I like walking around out there. The gravel is definitely of granitic origin: a lot of tourmaline gravel, a lot of feldspar—the white and the pink feldspars, the cleaved crystals. It's just a pretty sand and a pretty gravel. With that are all your micas that are inherently associated with your granites. It's a sparkling bed through the water, all the flat faces reflecting the sun."

Rawalt is a large, competent, confident man of the sort you'd expect to encounter if you were a halfback running a football. He has full cheeks, green eyes, and curly brown hair down over his forehead, flecking gray. His shirts button down. His suits are conservative, and rumpled from the road. He has a dark tie with Disney characters on it playing golf. Years ago, he testified in a Mississippi assault trial after police reluctantly mailed soil samples to the F.B.I. The police had accused a man of stalking a former girlfriend and shooting her through a window of her house, maiming her, after which, they surmised, he ran a mile to his car. The Mississippi police sent Rawalt a number of soil samples without saying which was which or where any of them were from, or telling him much of the story. They included samples from under the car. They included soil from the knee of the defendant's pants, which he had apparently smeared when he fell, running. Rawalt's report singled out the knee stain and matched it to the topography. It labelled the other samples and described the actions they implied. When he arrived in Mississippi to testify, a sheriff generously said to him, "You convinced us. You separated the soils and you told us which soil came from the wheel rut, and you also showed that a mud puddle was splashed on afterward. And out of all those soil samples you picked the one that showed where his knee slid on the side of the hill. You convinced us."

Rawalt said, "What did you think I was going to do—lie for you?"

His name is pronounced "Ray Walt." He was born near Chadron, Nebraska, southeast of the Black Hills. ("I grew up playing in the White River Oligocene north of town, digging fossils.") At Chadron State College, in 1971, he wrote his senior thesis on the recataloguing of fossils. While he was doing graduate work in geology at Colorado State University, he heard that the government was looking for geologists to do mineral studies in Vietnam. He applied, was accepted, and then found out that "government" meant "C.I.A." and that the relevant geology was in enemy territory. He applied instead to the F.B.I.

The Justice Department's Drug Enforcement Administration was established at about the same time. Over the years, the D.E.A. would make frequent requests of F.B.I. geologists. "An airplane is found abandoned someplace. They want to know if it took off from a sandbar in a river in central Colombia, based on the sands there. Sometimes we've been able to do that, from soil on the underside of the aircraft that got kicked up in the wheel-well sand." In 1985, Rawalt was working at the F.B.I. in Washington when a D.E.A. agent was kidnapped in Guadalajara. It had been a street abduction in noonday sun, and witnesses said that two vehicles seemed to be involved—a Volkswagen Atlantic and a Mercury Gran Marquis. A month went by while the White House, the State Department, and half the agencies in Washington put great pressure on the Mexican government and the Mexican Federal Judicial Police to find the agent and resolve the case. Finally came the day when the television news was full of revelation. The bodies of the American agent Enrique Camarena Salazar and Alfredo Zavala Avelar, a pilot who helped him do clandestine surveillance, had been found on a ranch in Michoacán. There had been a shootout between police and a family named Bravo—small-scale drug runners, who owned the ranch. Every person on the ranch was killed in the raid—husband, wife, three sons. An M.F.J.P. officer had been killed. Rawalt watched the television coverage, and watched again as the story was repeated. In early morning, he went out to his mailbox for the newspaper, and stood there absorbing what it said. The footage from the scene had showed bodies lying on the ground and covered with sheets. To him it seemed obvious that someone had dumped them there, because they were not being excavated from a burial site. It was reported that the bodies had soil adhering to them and, with respect to the ground around them, the colors were not the same. The dirt on the bodies was dark, the soil of the ranchland light. "The authorities' side of the story was that the Federales, the M.F.J.P., had received a tip on where Camarena's buried body—that was the key word, 'buried' body—would be located. And they went there and found the bodies. Case solved and closed. This was a premier case. We wanted that body back. Alive or dead, we wanted Camarena back. The Mexicans had to come up with a way of returning the body in such a way that it would take the pressure off of them and get our government off their back. The Mexican federal police 'solved the case' through the location of the bodies and the execution of witnesses who would have said, 'We don't know anything about it.' "

Rawalt called F.B.I. headquarters and asked the switchboard to connect him to the United States Embassy in Mexico City. Eventually, he got through to a sleepy man—possibly an assistant to the Ambassador—and told him he felt that he could prove through the soil alone that Camarena had not been buried at the Bravo ranch. He believed that he could prove as well that the site of exhumation was nowhere near the Bravo ranch. He just needed the minerals—samples of the soils. He added, "I think it's an absolutely transparent ploy by the Mexican government to placate us. That's my goal—to show a coverup."

The Camarena story was extensively covered in every news medium, and it also served as the structural framework of an exhaustive study by Elaine Shannon called "Desperados: Latin Drug Lords, U.S. Lawmen, and the War America Can't Win" (Viking, 1988). A television movie was made from her book. Needless to say, I don't intend to encapsulate either the film or Shannon's five hundred pages but merely to offer as a supplement the details of the forensic geology. Trials resulting from the Camarena case continued into the nineteen-nineties. The United States, doing all it could to bring accomplices before American juries, arrested people north of the border when opportunities arose. Eight were tried on charges that included murder. Forensic evidence of various kinds resulted in seven convictions. Until the trials were over, Rawalt and his geological colleagues refused all interviews about the subject.

"Next thing I know, it's Monday morning and I'm up in my assistant director's front office and he wants to know where I got this theory of a coverup. He has heard from the Department of State, and he is asking me to explain where I am getting this all-encompassing knowledge from that I am making these phone calls to Mexico. I admitted what I had done. He said, 'It would be nice if you would let us know before you make these wild calls. It's been discussed at the White House. But it seems like people agree that you've put your finger on what's going on, and if you think you can do something it's your case. You're going to be going to Mexico as soon as the soil samples get back here and you can do a comparison. Pick your team—anybody you want. D.E.A. will coöperate. They'll get you in and out of the country.' "

The samples were collected in the Guadalajara morgue by an F.B.I. agent named Jack Dillon, posing as a D.E.A. agent. From Camarena's skin, and from his clothing nearby, Dillon took about a teaspoon of earth. Camarena's body had been found in a state of advanced decomposition. In arid ground, dehydrating, it had begun to undergo the process known as mummification. The skin resembled leather. In his skull was a double concave fracture, resembling broken glass. Because of his ability to cultivate informants, Camarena—young, beefy, garrulous—had been one of the D.E.A.'s most effective agents.

In Washington, Rawalt looked at the samples. As he had read in the newspaper, the soil from Camarena's body was dark. It was actually wet. Adipose tissue had come through the skin and had caused the soil to stick together in small lumps. Moisture darkens soil, of course, and he needed to give the D.E.A. correct guidance on color, which he could not do without removing the fatty tissue from the minerals. Chemists at the F.B.I. had an oxygen plasma-reduction unit. In Rawalt's words, "It rusts body tissue. It causes carbon to rust. It replaces the oxygen radical for the carbon radical, burns the carbon radical off, and leaves a light-gray powder. It decomposes body material." A lump of the soil from Camarena's body spent eight hours in the plasma-reduction unit. "They've got oxygen set up with a pump, and they're evacuating the atmosphere, and doing all kinds of stuff, and—lo and behold—the thing came out ash gray. That was from the oxidation of the tissue. I used these little air pumps for dusting off optics. You could sit there and blow the gray away and see the soil underneath it. By systematically reducing the lump, a little bit at a time, and blowing the tissue away in the form of gray dust, I got down to the soil color. I'd never done that before, and to my knowledge it's never been done again." Color contrast was what had caused him, in the first place, to telephone the Embassy in Mexico City. Now, oddly, the contrast turned out to be the reverse of what had been reported. The rock of the Bravo soil, cleaned for inspection, was a globular obsidian, very dark greenish gray. The soil off the body was a sharp tuffaceous vesicular glass, tan to white in color. "There was a world of difference between the two. You didn't have to look at them for their mineral composition to know that these things were not even remotely close."

Rawalt, of course, did look at them for their mineral composition. The intended contribution of the forensic geology was to help guide the investigation, and to provide trial evidence if there ever was a trial. His immediate goals were to disprove the statement by the Mexican government that the Bravo ranch was the place where Camarena died and to suggest, if possible, where the body might have been buried. To do all that, he'd need more than contrasting colors.

The Bravo soil of Michoacán was no less volcanic than the soil on the body, but the volcanoes were different. The Bravo minerals were much coarser, heavier-grained, slug-like, rounded, and dirty (from trace substances trapped in the glass). There was not nearly as much ash. The globularity of the grains spoke of slow deposition in a sedimentary basin, of water deposits interlayered with ash flows from intermittent volcanic events. The soil from Camarena spoke of mountains.

Roughly ninety-eight per cent was tuffaceous wind-blown rhyolite ash. Rawalt's attention would settle on other components, which amounted to less than one per cent. The ash was very clean, high in silica, angular, vesicular. It had come out of a volcanic explosion as a fluid and had cooled suddenly as it sailed through the air. It could also be described as airfall pumice. Among the minor components of the Camarena soil were a notable concentration of bixbyite, blacker than coal, and a pink glass of exceptional depth and richness of color. ("I'd never seen anything quite like it, except in candy. I had worked with pink garnet, pink zircons—they don't look the same.") Less in quantity—and therefore of greater forensic value—were two kinds of cristobalite: opalized and clear. You might wander all over central Mexico occasionally finding one or the other form of cristobalite. You'd be getting pretty warm if you found two. The cristobalite crystals were elongate and faceted—clear polygonal columns. Octahedrons. To Rawalt, they resembled branch coral. They had developed in the volcanic explosion when, as molten material, they were forced into the vesicles in the tuffaceous glass. "It's like filling a straw. And then it cools slowly, insulated by the glass, and it goes back into a crystalline state. The reason some is opalized is that there's a high percentage of water in it when it is crystallizing. A lot of the glass in Camarena's stuff actually had the cristobalite still inside it. Weathering mechanics can break the tuff, and then the cristobalite is freed. But a lot of the tuffaceous rhyolite glass had cristobalite still within it. You could see the vesicles full of cristobalite. For us, it was the big indicator."

Rawalt went to the library of the United States Geological Survey, in Reston, Virginia, and studied maps and scientific papers that related to the region of Guadalajara. He was looking for rhyolite sources in high ground, which for central Mexico was to some extent like looking for pavement in New York City. But you started with that, and then used the bixbyite, the cristobalite, the rose glass to narrow it down. His colleague Chris Fiedler once outlined the problem by saying, "Initially you have the whole country of Mexico in which to find where a teaspoon of soil came from." In the *Journal of Volcanology & Geothermal Research*, Rawalt found a thirty-one-page paper by Gail Mahood, then of Berkeley, now of Stanford, on the "Geological Evolution of a Pleistocene Rhyolitic Center—Sierra La Primavera, Jalisco, Mexico." With its maps, charts, and cross-sections, it widened his eyes from the abstract onward. It described the types of sedimentary soil he was looking for: the airfall pumice, the caldera-lake sediments that would contain the pinkish material.

He went to the Smithsonian to review with the mineralogists there the results of his mineral studies. He was referred to a young woman who had done volcanological field work in the Guadalajara area and was at the Smithsonian at the time. As Rawalt began to explain the mineralogy he was working with, and mentioned the unusual hue of the rose glass, she immediately said that she recognized what he was talking about and that the minerals were specific to a Jalisco state park called Bosques de la Primavera. "She said, 'This is Primavera-park soil. This red-pink-type glass that you're talking about is a result of a third-event caldera formation. It was not extensive. It was confined just to the park and its slopes—the mountain itself.' And then we take the map, and she highlights the outcrops of rhyolite that will be upslope and in general conjunction with the mineralogy I'm looking for."

Not long after Rawalt turned in his results, he was called to the assistant director's office and told that he and three forensic scientists in other disciplines were to go to Mexico as soon as possible. "That meant, 'Do not go home and pack. Go to the airport right now. D.E.A. is waiting. They have an aircraft in Dallas. They're going to take you in.' We picked up stores from the disaster squad—clothing and stuff—downstairs. I took a small microscope, sufficient chemicals, cleansing solutions, and instruments. In Dallas, we got on a D.E.A. aircraft. It was a twin-engine turboprop, but its ground speed was about five hundred miles an hour. We hit the border and that pilot put that plane right on the desert, and we flew down under the Mexican radar. We went into a canyon a lot bigger than the Grand Canyon. We flew below the rims of other canyons, too. We landed in Guadalajara. We did not have permission to come into the country. F.B.I. was not allowed in the country. D.E.A. was. We were not to admit our identity. The D.E.A. bribed the Mexican customs officials—paid them cash not to look in our bags and not to ask who we were and why we were there, paid them cash just openly, right there at the airport." The twin-engine turboprop had been seized in the United States. It had belonged to a Mexican drug trafficker of the first order, whose name was Rafael Caro Quintero.

Rawalt stayed at the Hyatt Regency, in downtown Guadalajara. On his first night there, an officer of the Mexican Federal Judicial Police knocked on the door of his room. Rawalt opened the door. The M.F.J.P. man greeted him warmly and told him that he was in charge of making sure that Rawalt and the others were comfortable. "He wanted to know what I wanted. Did I need a little cocaine? Did I need a woman? Did I need a young boy? What did I want? He was to get it for me. I told him he had the wrong room and shut the door in his face."

A connotative beginning with Mexican authority. In the concentrated effort to solve the case of the American agent, the Drug Enforcement Administration's principal official colleagues were local, state, and federal Mexican police, not to mention government ministers and the Federal Security Directorate, or D.F.S. (D.F.S. = C.I.A.) As Elaine Shannon's "Desperados" documents thoroughly, especially with reference to Mexico, there was not a government agency, in law enforcement or otherwise, that did not in some way repose in the drug economy. In the war on drugs, it was impossible to tell from a uniform which side the wearer represented. With respect to who was and who was not being enriched by drug traffickers, the collective personnel in the list above were like shaken salt and sugar. A D.F.S. badge could quell inquiry anywhere in the country. The drug traffickers easily bought D.F.S. badges. "It's the top form of identification," Rawalt once said. "They paid millions and millions of dollars for their people to be issued these badges, so they could run through the country with impunity. They didn't have to worry about anybody stopping them." They could snatch an American agent off a street, hold him prisoner, torture him, crush his skull, and dispose of the body, even in the presence of "authorities." More than one M.F.J.P. officer was to tell Rawalt that Camarena had died of natural causes.

The intense American interest shown in Camarena's disappearance seems to have been baffling from the Mexican point of view. Others had vanished who were presumed American agents and much less fuss resulted. Americans had gone into Mexico never to be heard from again, and the news media did not seem to care. Scarcely a week before Camarena was kidnapped, a couple of Americans named Alberto Radelat and John Walker happened into a traffickers' party in a Guadalajara restaurant. The traffickers took them for D.E.A. agents infiltrating the neighborhood and tortured them and killed them. This had not produced a similar hue and cry. Eight weeks earlier, four American missionaries going door to door in Guadalajara had lifted the wrong latch. Drug-enforcement agents in California had been known to pose as geologists, so who was it that these missionaries were working for? They disappeared and their bodies were not to be found. In all, six American presumed agents had been killed by the traffickers in recent weeks. So why were the White House, the State Department, and the American press creating so much pressure now? "When this firestorm hit, the Mexicans didn't understand what was going on," Rawalt says. "They had killed seven, and we were interested in just one." In Guadalajara, Rawalt was asked in English by a mid-level officer of the M.F.J.P. to explain to him what the problem was. "I explained to him that in our country when you kill a law-enforcement officer it incenses the American public and becomes an important case. When you kill a federal agent, it incenses the American public. And we don't stand for that. He said he could not understand what the big deal was, because, he told me, in the M.F.J.P. they lost about two hundred officers a year in drug shootouts and retaliation murders. To them, it was a way of life."

It was believed that Camarena's unauthorized flights over marijuana fields in Chihuahua had led to incendiary raids and the destruction of a crop worth three hundred million dollars. The two marijuana-and-cocaine traffickers who had lost the most were Rafael Caro Quintero (former owner of the airplane that carried Rawalt under the rim-rocks into Mexico) and Ernesto Fonseca Carrillo. From Day One, they were seen as the principal perpetrators of Camarena's disappearance. On Day Three, Caro Quintero had left Mexico, seen off at the airport by Armando Pavón Reyes, *primer comandante* of the M.F.J.P., who, it turned out, received three hundred thousand dollars for letting him go. When the American firestorm was burning high and the White House was calling and the State Department was calling and the American press was swarming, a hundred Mexican troops surrounded a house where Fonseca was staying in Puerto Vallarta. A deafening gunfight began. It went on and on. It did not stop until the traffickers ran out of ammunition. When the smoke cleared, no one on either side had been hit. Fonseca, thereby captured, was jailed but not charged. A swat team snatched Caro Quintero from a villa in Costa Rica. Fonseca, of raptor face, was said to be a billionaire. The boyish curly-haired Caro Quintero could not have been worth more than five hundred million. They were incarcerated together in Mexico City in large comfortable rooms, where they kept fighting roosters and an arsenal of guns, gave parties with visiting female friends, and had their own chefs. In Rawalt's words, "They were being maintained by the Mexican government away from access by the American government."

Rawalt showed the D.E.A. investigators his maps and charts and mineralogy, and told them about the cristobalites and the rose glass. "These guys are— They don't know what I'm talking about. But they were convinced enough." With his hand in motion over a Jalisco state map, he said, "Here's where the guy was buried, right around this park. This is where we look. We don't go there, because this is where he is going to be." The most immediate effect of the mineralogy was to enable the D.E.A. to confront the Mexican government with evidence that the body had been moved and that the M.F.J.P.'s story of Bravo ranch was a fiction. When, or if, the true burial site was found, it would be up to Rawalt to match exactly the minerals of the site to the teaspoon of earth taken from the body—to present the forensic evidence matching body to grave. The D.E.A. had hypnotized a witness who had seen Camarena being beaten in a car heading south beyond the Guadalajara *periférico* (beltway). Under hypnosis, he remembered a part of the license plate. The D.E.A. wanted Rawalt to go south. "But the geology didn't match. It was not the right kind of soil. I did not have these large rhyolitic extrusions influencing the soil factors. We spent minimal time down there." Mexican television and newspapers were full of the story, and people were calling in and writing in to say where Camarena had been held and where he had been buried, and even to report seeing him alive. The tips on burial sites included Cancún, the Chihuahuan desert, and scattered stations along the primary cocaine-marijuana route through the west and north. The D.E.A. wanted Rawalt to check out these places. Rawalt resisted such coverage as often as he could. ("I'm convinced from the geology that we've got the area located. For me to convince myself to look somewhere else, I've got to duplicate what I already know is in their back yard. And killers are lazy. Why would they take a guy clear to northern Mexico to get rid of a body?")

He went first, of course, to the Bosques de la Primavera, a fire-swept country, arid six to nine months a year, where pine needles are exceptionally thin. Michael Malone, who had flown with him from Washington and was an expert in things like carpet fibres and hair, went along to assist him and to be with him if trouble should arise. The M.F.J.P. did not know that they were out there, let alone that they were F.B.I. "We were not to go anywhere without an M.F.J.P. escort. That was part of the rules of engagement, so to speak. We didn't trust them. We were well armed."

Malone and Rawalt had a pickup. In likely places, they put the tailgate down, and Rawalt set up a lab. "I could use a nonpolarized scope and immediately make a determination based on the cristobalite. If I'd been using some of the other indicating features, I would have had to have a pole scope to identify the minerals. I did have a small pole scope, but I was using ambient light. We had no power sources that we could hook up that scope to. The easy indicator was the cristobalite. We might pick thirty samples. We'd wash them up. We'd take a quick look at them under the microscope. For one reason or another, we'd eliminate them. What we tried to do was ballpark an area. We were looking for those key cristobalites and rose-colored-glass features. We started on the mountainside, up high. In soft soil, we started getting samples from the surface and a foot down and two feet down, looking for these things. I eliminated roughly four hundred soil samples. They just weren't the same. They were close. We had the type of glass. In some of them we had cristobalites—but not as much as we needed. Or we'd have rose glass with no cristobalite. Or we'd have the glass but we wouldn't have the rhyolite. And we had to have them all. We did ditches, ravines, sides of roads. We went clear into the hot springs." In three days, they covered about twenty square miles. The Forest of Primavera was a few thousand square miles.

An informant told the D.E.A. that a Mercury Gran Marquis was sealed up behind a fresh wall of adobe across the front of a residential garage near the southern boundary of the park. Rawalt and four other F.B.I. agents went there and did a crime scene. There was blood in the car. Hair on a floor mat and on the back of the front seat matched hair that Jack Dillon had removed from Camarena in the morgue. The car derived from one of Caro Quintero's Mercury-Ford dealerships. Rawalt looked for the story that might be written on the undercarriage, but all he found were fine silts from numerous locations.

They went to Michoacán for a wider test of the Bravo

ranchland. The ranch house was not a prototype of Mexican rural architecture. It had barred windows, gun slits, and walls half a metre thick. It was a fort. There were enough big bullet holes in the walls to house a flock of purple martins.

Malone and Rawalt were assigned, as "D.E.A. agents," to check out various addresses associated with Fonseca and Caro Quintero. On such missions, the M.F.J.P. was supposed to accompany them. "By their actions, the M.F.J.P. told us how dangerous it was. When we'd go to a search, they'd disappear. They might escort you up there, but when it came to going into a house or going into a compound they disappeared. They were there for our protection, and to help us, yet they were absolutely working a hundred and eighty degrees from us at all times." Balking, the M.F.J.P. would point out the need for a search warrant. ("Don't even mention Mexico and a search warrant in the same breath.") The M.F.J.P. also warned that the houses and compounds could be full of *pistoleros*. Approaching a walled compound, Rawalt, Malone, and a couple of D.E.A. agents would knock, and when no one answered they'd open the place and gingerly go in. "We're talking about a fifteen-bedroom mansion with indoor pool, outdoor pool, and a twelve-foot-high wall—a compound with lights, and cameras on the corners, encompassing three to four acres, with big interior vegetable gardens, and servant quarters—like a small Alamo. We're armed to the teeth. I had a MAC 10—a little submachine gun—and a 9-mm. pistol. Mike had a handgun. When you're out, you're dressed with a machine gun and with a handgun. You were told that in essence you cannot trust anybody but the D.E.A. Your life is at danger. Do not go to dinner. Do not go for a job without going in groups. An easy way to tell the good guys from the bad guys down there was by the armament they were carrying.

M.F.J.P. officers are very open about to whom they owe their allegiance. If you're carrying an AK-47 rifle, that rifle comes up through Central America to the drug traffickers. That's where they get their weapons, and they pass the weapons on. One of the first things we looked for with the people who were supposedly guarding us and helping us was the type of weapons they were carrying. Here's an M.F.J.P. officer, and look what he's carrying—an AK-47. This is just flaunting the fact that he is there protecting the people in the drug trade—he's a traffickers' *pistolero*, he's also an M.F.J.P. officer. Time was danger down there. You hit a trafficker's house and the trafficker knew it—through the M.F.J.P. or through the peons who were working there who had taken off when we pulled up. Wasted time could mean a carload of *pistoleros* coming down the road for a gunfight."

In one compound, Malone was doing his fibre collecting and Rawalt his soil sampling when the M.F.J.P. appeared. Seeing that no one had been killed and no *pistoleros* were present, they entered the house. For three hours, while Malone and Rawalt went on collecting and sampling, the M.F.J.P. systematically rifled the place. They stole all the liquor, the food in the pantry, the television sets, and the parabolic dish off the top of the house. They took clothing, shoes, silverware. They pried a safe out of a wall. Rawalt and two D.E.A. agents were working in an upstairs room when a shot was fired. All three hit the floor, imagining forty *pistoleros*. Silence. Guns drawn, they got up warily and looked around. They looked out a window. The M.F.J.P. had shot a pig. They were putting it into the trunk of a car. A whole line of cars was there, bumper to bumper, trunks open, being loaded with household goods.

One day, the federal paradoxical police informed the D.E.A. that they had learned where Camarena had been held. The address was in central Guadalajara—881 Lope de Vega. Rawalt and Malone were asked to do the crime scene, as part of a D.E.A. team. When they arrived, NBC, ABC, and CBS were on the curb. There were trucks with dishes pointed at the sky. Rawalt recalls his reaction when he first glimpsed the house and compound: "It's a logical place to hold a person. Because what's it look like? It looks like a jail." The walls were eighteen-inch adobe. Every window was blocked by white-painted iron bars. The doors, inches thick, were reinforced with metal strapping. After the house, courtyard, guesthouse, arcade, and swimming pool came a tennis court bordered with jaguars. These were not motorcars. They were living black and spotted jaguars, in six cages. Also beside the tennis court was a Volkswagen Atlantic with no license plates.

Indoors, fresh paint was on most of the wall space, entombing fingerprints. Rooms had been swept spotless. The main power line had been cut. "They knew we processed with vacuum cleaners—they'd seen us doing it at other houses. We put on heavy gloves and spliced the ends—hooked those babies together and taped them up with evidence tape." Still no power. The fuses, which were of the screw-in type, had all been removed. This was late in the day, light fading. Rawalt put copper coins in the fuse sockets and rammed them in with the wooden handle of a mop. Every coin welded. The lights now worked. They turned on their vacuum cleaner.

The lawn had been completely raked, but a pile of leaves had been left there. Among the leaves was an order to the commandant of the M.F.J.P. to supply ammunition to the drug traffickers. The water in the pool was opaque. Rawalt explored the bottom with a broom handle. It was overrun with bottles and cans. Water would not erase fingerprints. Rawalt asked the M.F.J.P. for a pump from a firehouse. The M.F.J.P. said no. He found a pump in the pool house, rigged it up, and started it. An M.F.J.P. officer kicked the pump into the pool. Before anyone could return with another pump, the pool had been emptied and scrubbed.

The guesthouse was a cell within a fort, with its own barred windows and a half-inch boilerplate door. The vacuum cleaner picked up hair from the guesthouse carpet that would match Camarena's. In the bathroom, the lower six feet of tile was bright and clean. The tiles above were grimy. Among traffickers who sought information or confession from a captive, a routine method of torture was Tickle the Bone. Icepicks are run into knee joints, elbows, vertebrae, and elsewhere and then scraped on the bone. There was the Pepsi Challenge. Rawalt's description: "Tie a person to a chair, shake up a bottle of Pepsi, and shove it up the nose. Shooting that into your lungs under high pressure gives you the sensation of drowning. You'll confess to anything. Yet there's no scars or marks. I asked one of the M.F.J.P. officers if they really used that treatment, and he says, 'Of course not. We don't use Pepsi or Coke. They stain your clothes. We use seltzer water.' " An informant eventually told the D.E.A. that a doctor had assisted in the interrogation of Camarena. The doctor had used painkillers, so the traffickers could stretch out the beating and questioning. After a dry-cleaning bag was used to suffocate Camarena and take him near death, the doctor would be there to revive him. Rawalt found a cleaning bag in a closet, and an acid bottle as well. Evidently, the prisoner had been burned with acid.

Rounding a stair landing in the main house, Rawalt suddenly felt an M16 in his stomach, prodding. He was prodded to admit that he was not a D.E.A. agent, that he was really from the F.B.I. He didn't admit.

On the day of Camarena's abduction, an M.F.J.P. officer had used the Volkswagen to pick up some dry cleaning. He was given a dated receipt. He slipped the receipt under the weather sealing of the VW's trunk, where Rawalt now found it. In the trunk was blood that matched Camarena's and two strands of his hair.

In a drain beside the tennis court, Rawalt noticed a license plate folded in half. He asked for a crowbar to lift the grating. Alarmed and hostile, an M.F.J.P. officer refused. A crowbar was improvised, and the grating was lifted. The M.F.J.P. radioed for backup. The Americans photographed the license plate. Federales came in force and demanded the plate. Rawalt refused. He describes the situation as "a classical Mexican standoff," and continues the story: "Their guns were off their shoulders. I was told by our legate, 'You have no choice, turn it over to them.'" Beyond the caged jaguars Rawalt noticed *pistoleros*, their guns trained on him. Mike Malone, seeing the confrontation, had begun to worry about losing collected evidence. While the M.F.J.P. and Rawalt were squared off by the pool, Malone was loading evidence into a D.E.A. truck. An agent drove the truck to the American Consulate and locked the evidence in a vault.

Rawalt and Malone were kicked out of Mexico. They had made a mistake no less risible than leaving indicative orders in a pile of leaves. They had used F.B.I. evidence tape. They were taken to the airport and put on a jet, Air Mexicana. Nearing the United States border at thirty thousand feet, the pilot unexpectedly announced that they were going to have to land at the Mexican airbase at Loreto. Malone and Rawalt looked at each other and put their passports and badges and other identification in the foam of several seats. The plane touched down. The passengers were herded into a thatched hut with a corrugated roof. An army officer explained through an interpreter that in order to leave the country each passenger had to pay eight American dollars. Rawalt listed it on his expense voucher as "highjacking fee."

Some months earlier, a representative of a California aerospace company had approached the F.B.I. in behalf of the company's French consultant, Loic Le Ribault. The representative said that Le Ribault was the head petrologist for the French national oil company, had his own aerospace group, and was very wealthy. He wanted to get into forensics, because he could do things to solve cases that other people could not do. Show him a few grains of sand and he could tell you where they were from. He had tried to interest the national crime laboratories of France and Great Britain but had failed. He felt sure that if the F.B.I. showed interest others would follow. He called his work exoscopy.

The F.B.I. said, "A few grains?"

Le Ribault's representative said, "Test him. Just test him. Give me three samples."

While the man waited, the F.B.I. geologists—Fiedler, Rawalt, and others—conferred. Into a pillbox they put some ash from Mt. St. Helens. Into another they put alluvium from a river delta in South Carolina that related to a recent murder. What to put into the third pillbox? Across the hall were some girders from the Marine Corps barracks that was bombed in Beirut. Rawalt remembered noticing that dirt had been blasted into the girders. He scraped some out and boxed it.

A few weeks later, a spiral binder arrived from La Teste de Buch, a town in the Médoc. The cover said "Exoscopic Study of 3 Samples of Sands, by Loic Le Ribault." It was vintage stuff, so good it was hard to swallow. The F.B.I. had collected samples of Mt. St. Helens ash from all over the

West to record size and particle distribution and depositional cycles, because the ash would become a factor in soils
at crime scenes. Le Ribault's study said that Sample 1 was
Mt. St. Helens ash and had been deposited on an angle
within a hundred miles of the volcano. "He hit it within a
couple of miles," Rawalt says. "We called the senior resi-
dent agent who collected the ash and said, 'Where'd you
get it?' He says, 'It was on the hood of my car. I was parked
out there on a slope.' " Sample 2, according to Le Ribault's
report, came from a river basin in the American Southeast
and with geologic maps of sufficient scale the location could
be pointed out. The third sample was baffling, the report
admitted, and what follows here is Rawalt's paraphrase of
what Le Ribault wrote: "It's a pyroclastic event, a deposit
under extreme force—an explosion. It can only be a short
time since the deposition of this grain on a vertical surface.
I have no idea where this one comes from, because the only
place I can match this mineral grain to—any place in the
world that I can find—is in the Bekáa Valley in Lebanon,
and of course the F.B.I. does not do cases in Lebanon. So
I have no idea where it comes from." After the F.B.I. geologists had finished reading the report, someone said, "We
need to talk to this man."

Rawalt remembers Le Ribault as "a short little guy,
early fifties, very jovial, with sharp features, who talked a
mile a minute." Le Ribault brought an interpreter with him
to the F.B.I.'s Forensic Science Research and Training Center, in Quantico, Virginia. In a scanning electron microscope, he looked at quartz from Camarena's body—ordinary
quartz, out of the rhyolite. He blew it up ten thousand times
and read the sign on its surfaces. Water dissolves quartz,
slowly but certainly. Water leaching into soil dissolves some
of the quartz in a mineral grain, and as the silica-rich solution dries off it recrystallizes. In supermagnification, you

can see the subcrystallization, as the surface change is called, and as the subcrystallization varies it tells varying stories. If it is all over the grain, the grain was deposited in water. If it is on the top of the grain at such-and-such an angle, the mountainside was steep there. "He'll take a single grain and tell you the angle of deposition, how long it's been there, and where it comes from," Rawalt continues. "He also looks at the solubility of the quartz, and he looks at the surfaces to see how much they've been eroded by water. From his experience, he can tell you the nature of the exposure to environmental factors, and from his experience he makes a conclusion. The knowledge of how quartz dissolves and recrystallizes is the basis for his whole exoscopy science."

During the week that Le Ribault spent at Quantico, earth samples kept pouring in from the D.E.A. in Mexico —all negative. Standing before the scanning electron microscope—on its screen a quartz grain like a large map —Le Ribault said, "You have a rhyolite outcrop up a slope."

Rawalt said, "Yes, we've already figured that out."

Le Ribault had been given three of the samples that Rawalt had collected in the Forest of Primavera, as well as earth from Camarena's body. On a map Rawalt showed Le Ribault where he had collected the samples. Le Ribault said, "You're there, but not quite. You're at about the right elevation in the park, and at about the right angle of slope on which this quartz grain was deposited. The style of deposition and the depth are right. You're there, but you're not there. These are from an area washing north. The burial site was in an area washing south." Le Ribault continued, "This rhyolitic-base sand was deposited by water. It was deposited around four to five feet deep. The crystallography says that it came from a draw. The slope of the draw is less than ten degrees. Shade predominates there. When you go back, it may help to note that the outcrop this sand derives from is four thousand feet above the site where the body was buried."

Le Ribault made a large contribution to Rawalt's confidence and, with regard to the story that Camarena had been killed and buried at the Bravo ranch, he underscored the Mexican farce. At increased volume, the D.E.A. could repeat to the M.F.J.P. that their scenario was phony. The D.E.A., in need of continuing guidance from the forensic work of the F.B.I., pleaded with the Mexican government to let Malone and Rawalt return to the country as acknowledged F.B.I. agents—Rawalt to continue working in the Bosques de la Primavera. No response was forthcoming. Then a D.E.A. agent in Mexico called Washington to say, "We have Radelat and Walker's pit, or are going to." The D.E.A. had a new informant, who said he could show them where the car had been parked when the bodies of the Americans had been carried into the forest. The assistant director of the F.B.I. Laboratory appealed directly to the Attorney General of Mexico to permit Rawalt and Malone to return. The Attorney General's reply was that Rawalt could come but Malone could not. Rawalt speculates that the Mexicans were made especially uneasy by Malone's carpet work—his vacuum cleaner, his hair-and-fibre work—but could not imagine being inconvenienced by anything a geologist might do.

The site was on a southerly slope in Primavera, up a thoroughfare that resembled a mule trail more than a road. A short distance into the forest was a draw, a wash, its gradient less than ten degrees. It was shaded by tall trees. To the immediate north, and four thousand feet above, were extensive rhyolite outcrops. The rainy season had arrived. The air was densely humid and hot. A stench of human and animal decay was high enough to jam the throat. A horse rotting there looked like a balloon. The M.F.J.P. were already on the scene, with backhoe. Its bucket had disassembled the bodies of Radelat and Walker as it scooped them out. The digging had reached about five and a half feet down when Rawalt arrived. Seeing the backhoe, he thought, Nice forensic tool. Some ribs, vertebrae, and tissue were still in the pit. Rawalt removed them by hand. The M.F.J.P., a dozen in number and dead drunk, were engaged in a competitive game that involved cutting down the fine-needle pines with machine guns. Ammunition was everywhere. So potent were the smells of lead, cordite, powder, and decay that Rawalt had instantly developed a headache.

He supposed that Camarena and the pilot, Zavala, had been buried on top of Radelat and Walker. To compare mineralogies, he took soil samples from ground level down to the bottom of the pit. He set up his microscope and looked. At five feet, there was only a slight difference from the mineral suite off Camarena's body. "There was a little bit too much iron content in that pit. A small lens of iron-rich sediment ran through there from an old dry streambed."

When the D.E.A. had called Washington to report on their latest informant, they had said that he knew where people had left the road carrying Radelat's and Walker's bodies but did not know exactly where the bodies were buried. There might be a need for dogs. The F.B.I. does not have cadaver dogs. Rawalt called a training center and learned the whereabouts of America's five best teams of cadaver dogs. From Tuscaloosa, Alabama, a team was soon in the air. On the ground in Primavera, they were initially useless. "Cadaver dogs work hungry," Rawalt explains. "They locate a cadaver because they like the smell and they like the taste. Their reward is to eat part of the 'proud flesh'—the remains. So they work hungry. The dogs that first day were just listless as hell. It turned out someone had fed them. All the dogs were just gorged on dog food."

Cadaver dogs work singly as well as hungry. On the following day, the first dog released showed attention to a small depression some yards up the draw from Radelat and Walker's open grave. The animal dug a little. It did not give a clear signal, but a new pit was worth trying. The pervasive odors of dead bodies made it all but impossible for a dog to be unambiguous about a location so near. During the digging, Rawalt took samples at ground level and down through six or seven soil horizons. As the depth of the pit approached five feet, there was fresh high smell. If this was where Camarena had been buried, the opalescent and the clear cristobalite would be present in equal amounts. Under his microscope, as sample followed sample, that is what he saw. Given the two cristobalites, in balance, the next indicating feature would be the rose-colored quartz. It had the rhombohedral shape of a sugar crystal. He even wondered if, somehow, sugar was what he was looking at. He culled out some crystals and tried to dissolve them. They would not dissolve. What he was seeing in his microscope was not candy. "Almost pink-red, usually a negative crystal, it was just brilliant." The slight difference was no longer there. He was matching the soil that Jack Dillon had removed from Camarena's body in the morgue.

DUTY

OF

CARE

.

The world's largest pile of scrap tires is not visible from Interstate 5, in Stanislaus County, California. But it's close. Below Stockton, in the region of Modesto and Merced, the highway follows the extreme western edge of the flat Great Central Valley, right next to the scarp where the Coast Ranges are territorially expanding as fresh unpopulated hills. The hills conceal the tires from the traffic. If you were to abandon your car three miles from the San Joaquin County line and make your way on foot southwest one mile, you would climb into steeply creased terrain that in winter is jade green and in summer straw brown, and, any time at all, you would come upon a black vista. At rest on sloping ground, the tires are so deep that they form their own topography—their own escarpments, their own overhanging cliffs. Deposited from a ridgeline, they border a valley for nearly half a mile. When you first glimpse them, you are not sure what they are. From the high ground on the opposite side, the individual tires appear to be grains of black sand. They look like little eggstones—oolites—each a bright yolk ringed in black pearl. Close to them, you walk in tire canyons. In some places, they are piled six stories high, compressing themselves, densifying: at the top, tires; at the bottom, pucks. From the highest elevations of this thick and drifted black mantle, you can look east a hundred miles and see snow on the Sierra.

The tires are from all sides of the bays of San Francisco and up and down the Great Central Valley from Bakersfield to Sacramento. Even before the interstate was there, a tire jockey named Ed Filbin began collecting them—charging dealers and gas stations "tipping fees" of so much per passenger tire and so much per truck tire, as tire jockeys everywhere do. This was long before people began to worry, with regard to used tires, about mosquitoes, fires, landfills, and compounding environmental concerns, or to look upon old tires as a minable resource. Filbin's pile just grew, and he made enough money to diversify, becoming, as he is today, the largest sheep rancher in Nevada. Meanwhile, his tire ranch near Modesto continued to broaden and thicken, until no one, including Filbin, knew how many tires were there. Eventually, the state took notice—and county zoning authorities—and Filbin felt harassed. When I called him one day in Nevada, he sketched these people as "dirty rotten bureaucrats" and said, "I told them to go jump in a crick. I had grandfather rights." With those words, he cradled his telephone, refusing to say more.

There have been many estimates of the number of tires in the great California pile, but the figures tend to be high or low in direct proportion to the appraiser's economic interest or environmental bias. The variations can be absurd, missing agreement with one another by factors as high as five. Not long ago, while I was at the University of California, Davis, working on something else, I began to muse about the tire pile and the problem of counting its contents. In the university library I found David Lundquist, the map librarian, and asked for his suggestions. The pile does not appear on the 7.5-minute Solyo Quadrangle of the United States Geological Survey, and I thought he might have a more sophisticated map of equally ample scale. He said he had recent low-altitude aerial photographs made by the federal Agricultural Stabilization and Conservation Service that amounted to an eyeball-to-earth mosaic of the state. The prints were nine by ten and were in several map-cabinet drawers. Comparing map and photograph indexes, he rummaged through stacks of pictures. When No. 507-52 was at last before us, a shape in black Rorschach, sharply defined, stood out like a mountain lake. The terrain was veiny with clear draws and ridgelines, which made relatively simple the task of re-creating the dark shape on a copy of the Solyo topographic map. To help determine the acreage covered, a Davis geologist gave me a piece of graph paper whose squares were so small that four thousand four hundred and twenty-two of them covered one square mile on the map. Having seen the great pile and moved around it close, I could assign it an average thickness. Jack Waggoner, of Sacramento, who has spent his career as a distributor of tire-retreading and tire-shredding equipment, supplied figures for average densities of tires compressed by their own weight. On its side, a tire occupies about four square feet. A calculator blended these facts. While I had read or been given estimates of eight, nine, fifteen, twenty-five, forty-two, and forty-four, the calculator was reporting that in the world's largest known pile there are thirty-four million tires.

You don't have to stare long at that pile before the thought occurs to you that those tires were once driven upon by the Friends of the Earth. They are not just the used tires of bureaucrats, ballplayers, and litter-strewing rock-deafened ninja-teen-aged nyrds. They are everybody's tires. They are Environmental Defense Fund tires, Rainforest Action Network tires, Wilderness Society tires. They are California Natural Resources Federation tires, Save San Francisco Bay Association tires, Citizens for a Better Environment tires. They are Greenpeace tires, Sierra Club tires, Earth Island Institute tires. They are Earth First! tires! No one is innocent of scrapping those tires. They who carry out what they carry in have not carried out those tires. Of the problem the tire pile represents, everybody is the cause, and the problem, like the pile, has been increasing. (The California Integrated Waste Management Board has referred to the state's "growing tire population.") Most landfills across the country are refusing tires now, because most landfills are filling up, and, moreover, tires "float." They won't stay covered up. They work their way to the surface like glacial rocks. Intended by their manufacturers to be reliable and durable, they most emphatically are. Nothing about an automobile is safer than its tires, whose ultimate irony is that when they reach the end of their intended lives they are all but indestructible. When they are thrown away, they are just as tough as they were when they felt Kick One. On the surface or underground or on the beds of rivers, they don't decay. They are one per cent of all municipal solid waste and symbol of the other ninety-nine. Locked into the chemistry of each passenger tire is more than two and a half gallons of recoverable petroleum. California by itself discards twenty million tires a year. The United States throws away two hundred and fifty million tires a year. Strewn about the country at last count are something like three billion trashed tires. A hundred and seventy-eight million barrels of oil.

In southern Connecticut, beside a meander bend of the Quinnipiac River, a large privately owned landfill includes a thirty-acre body of water known as the Tire Pond. It was once a quarry, a clay pit. The town line between Hamden and North Haven runs through it. For a decade or so, the tire jockey Joe Farricielli has been tipping tires into the water there. He collects from more than two hundred customers, almost all in Connecticut, who pay him sixty-five cents to take an ordinary tire and as much as five dollars to be rid of a large one. The Tire Pond, now about half full, contains fifteen million tires.

When I made a visit there, the place was managed by Jim Rizzo, vice-president of the Tire Pond. His office was a small brick structure landscaped with young spruce that were standing in the centers of tires. Rizzo was an easy-talking, slightly burly man with a dark and radial mustache, who would not have looked amiss teaching paleontology at Harvard. He was wearing bluejeans and a gray Lacoste pullover. It was an April morning, and out toward the pond we drove in his pickup past trailers newly arrived. Men were grading the tires in them—looking for "high treads," Rizzo said, to be resold. Up the road, the company used to have a retail outlet called Second Time Around. It was not a big success, but they still sell high treads for fifteen dollars at the pond. For California, Mexico is the second time around. California tire jockeys sell more than a million discarded tires in Mexico each year, where they are mounted on Mexicans' cars.

Now Rizzo and I were on a dirt road in what appeared to be a field of dry tires, eye high. There was open water beyond. He said that the tires were protruding above the surface of the pond and were resting on other tires, which went all the way to the bottom. They were standing in water as deep as or deeper than most of the Atlantic Ocean dump sites in the New York bight. In fact, if we were to go down the Quinnipiac and across Long Island Sound and across

Long Island to the ocean, we would have to go twenty miles out to sea to find a depth greater than the Tire Pond's. "After the tires get to be five or six feet above water, they are covered with geotextile fabric, and the fabric is then covered with clean fill—concrete, sand, stone, soil—two to three feet thick," Rizzo said. "That is the covering. Everything below that down to the bottom of the pond is tires. That covering is firm. In fact, you and I are now *on* the pond. We are driving on tires."

A large dump truck carrying seven hundred and fifty tires had also driven out upon the pond. It had stopped close to the rubber shoreline. A long stainless hydraulic shaft lifted one end of the bed. Seven hundred and fifty tires slid into the water. They looked like black ice cubes. Rizzo said that when tires are added they do not raise the level of the water. The excess just goes away. A tip is a place where material is dumped, as from wagons. This tip was what was left of the Stiles Brick Company, which in the nineteenth century and on into the twentieth had dug out two hundred thousand cubic yards of clay. The pond was a hundred and forty feet deep. No mosquitoes. No pests. No fires.

Soon after Joe Farricielli bought the landfill, in the middle nineteen-seventies, he experienced a tire fire, and that is what drew his attention to the potentialities of the pond. A tire fire sends off billows of stinking black acidulous smoke, which, drifting downwind full of polynuclear aromatic hydrocarbons, benzene, and other toxic pollutants, attracts the attention of neighbors, zoning boards, and departments of environmental protection. Tire jockeys can recite by heart the roll call of the great fires, including Platteville, Colorado, 1987, where the pile burned for four days; Hagersville, Ontario, 1990, where the pile burned for seventeen days; Palmetto, Georgia, 1992, where the fire burned for five weeks; and Winchester, Virginia, 1983–84, where the pile burned continuously for nine months. In the Virginia fire, seven million tires were involved. Tire-pile fires are usually the result of arson. In the pile at Sid's in Norton, Ohio, four fires occurred within six months. Typically, the arsonist fills tires with newspapers. The Tire Pond was beyond the reach of the New Haven *Register*, the Hartford *Courant*, and even the incendiary New York *Times*.

To the Hagersville fire, outside Toronto, in February of 1990, the London Fire Brigade sent an observer. He noted the efficacy of sand and chemicals, and the inadvisability of fighting such fires with water, which augments the toxic spill. Where not much oxygen is involved, a burning tire will decompose into carbon black, gas, and oil. A tire fire oozes oil. If water is used to fight the fire, the oil travels with it. The fluid then contaminates groundwater, surface water, and soil. In Winchester, Virginia, where the tire fire burned for two hundred and seventy-five days, the runoff was collected. It included six hundred and ninety thousand gallons of oil, which was sold for a hundred and eighty-four thousand dollars.

Mosquitoes? A tire that is under water is not breeding mosquitoes. A tire with a little rain in it is a near-perfect mosquito incubator, as any reader of *Mosquito News* or the *Journal of the American Mosquito Control Association* can tell you. Almost any old tire, dumped legally or not, can help disseminate vector-borne viral diseases—for example, La Crosse virus, dengue fever, Sepik fever, Ross River fever, Japanese encephalitis, St. Louis encephalitis. The concern is not just domestic. In the complexities of international economics, the United States annually imports three million used tires. About a quarter of them contain a little water and, often, some mosquito larvae. The tires are, in large part, for recapping and reshipping to other parts of the world, but some are rejected for retreading. They go into scrap heaps, and the mosquitoes stay here. Most of the worn tires that arrive in ships come from Asian countries where *Aedes albopictus* is indigenous—a mosquito that can serve as a viral vector but by nature does not migrate and has a lifetime flight range of less than a thousand yards. In other words, this mosquito goes nowhere on its own. Used tires have dispersed it throughout the Western Hemisphere.

The State of Connecticut has checked the Tire Pond and found no *Aedes albopictus*, Rizzo said. Tires, moreover, are not exactly soluble; they don't affect the water. Since the pond's inception as a tire fill, it has had a water-compliance permit from the Department of Environmental Protection. As if to emphasize the tenor of Rizzo's presentation, two alabaster swans came into view, swimming on the Tire Pond. We were now beyond the filled area and beside the open water. We paused on the pond's eastern shore, on the isthmus that separated it from the Quinnipiac River. The view to the west was multilaminate and somewhat surreal. In the background, against the sky, was a hillside green with shade trees over spread-out suburban homes. The New Haven Country Club was up there somewhere, and Quinnipiac College, and Lake Whitney. The next layer, below, consisted of the light industries of State Street and a lengthy ribbon of a sign that said "Volkswagen, New and Used Cars." The stratum below that was Amtrak—New Haven to the left, Hartford to the right. The bottom layer was the Tire Pond, on its surface the Wagnerian swans, a couple of mallards, a few dozen gulls, and the black-sparkling ice-cube tires drifting about in the wind.

I was growing suspicious of Rizzo. The thought was occurring to me that he and Farricielli had imported the swans. In the bright sun, the birds seemed to blaze white. "We are members of the Audubon Society," Rizzo was say-

ing. "People from Audubon come here to count the birds.
Those ducks nest in the tires."

A day or two later, I would talk on the telephone with
Milan Bull, director of field studies and ornithology, Connecticut Audubon Society, who said that he always goes to
the Tire Pond at Christmas and at one or two other times
during the year. "Open spaces attract birds," he explained.
"They like the weeds there. Song sparrows, savanna sparrows, brushy-type birds. Meadowlarks. Occasional bobo-
links. Open-field birds. Orange-crowned warblers. The Tire
Pond is hit regularly during the Christmas count. Maybe
two hundred people go there a year. Birds are right in the
surface tires. Nests are in the tires—song sparrows', American goldfinches', I guess. We see mallards, pied-billed
grebes, wood ducks, the mute swans. Mute swans are an
increasing species in Connecticut. There has been a dra-
matic increase in ten years. There are about four thousand
across the state now. The swans don't nest in the Tire Pond,
but probably along the Quinnipiac River."

I also met Anne Evans at the Tire Pond. Jack Waggoner, in California, had strongly suggested that I call on
her. Born into the tire trade, in Middletown, Connecticut,
she had taken charge of her family's business at the age of
twenty-two, selling and mounting new tires and paying the
Middletown landfill to carry the old ones away. When she
was twenty-nine, she had become president of the New
England Association of Independent Tire Dealers. But now,
at thirty-seven, she had long since given up retailing tires
in order to concern herself full time with what might be
done to get rid of them—specifically, to develop profitable
ways of using them after they have fulfilled their initial

purpose. As a convenience to me, she had proposed meeting at the pond to talk tires, and had said that no matter what she might say to me it would not ruffle Jim Rizzo, because he had heard it all before. "The tire industry is really, really, really, really tiny," she had said. "We're a small industry. We all know one another. And we stick together."

Now, on that spring morning, as her dark bright eyes swept over Rizzo's establishment, she said, "At least it's not going to burn." She wore a blue-gray suit over an aquamarine blouse. Her dark glasses, tilted upward, nested in her short black hair. She wore gold earrings, a gold necklace, a sapphire bracelet, and a ring with a diamond as big as a tire. "This place is a blight on the earth," she went on. "They're making a fortune. They bought the clay pit for next to nothing. Their overhead is almost nothing. While other people are spending millions of dollars on equipment for recycling, they've got a hole. The tires will sit in the hole forever. To me it's just something so incredible that thirteen million tires are in a hole and no one cares!"

Someone muttered, "Fifteen million."

"This is the way things went for a long time," she continued. "Tires were just dumped, and no attempt was made to do something with them." The Tire Pond, like the rubber alp in California, had been what she called a "regional solution"—an innovative response to the choking of local landfills. "I guess this pond is not as bad as a pile of tires in a ravine," she concluded. "On the other hand, tires in a ravine can be removed. These are here for an eternity."

If I wanted to meet an authentic pioneer in doing something about tires, she said, I should go to Baltimore and look up Norman Emanuel. She added reverently, "He mastered the early shredding machines. He sells to energy users. He's done very, very well. And he's still in overalls."

My dialogue with Anne Evans was by no means exhausted, and her widespread insights and personal history would in various ways inform much of the rest of these notes. Meanwhile, I did as I was told. I went to inner Baltimore, just west of Amtrak, and found Bentalou Street, where—seeking, as I was, the preeminent tire shredder of eastern America—I expected to see begrimed industrial structures of the sort that are everywhere framed in the begrimed windows of Amtrak. Bentalou was a shade street, though, of maples, sycamores, ash, elms, lindens, flowering cherries. Its row houses had small lawns and covered fieldstone porches—an obvious escalation from the signature marble steps that spill with such perspective symmetry to wide sidewalks of Baltimore. On Bentalou were greening hedges, blossoming azaleas, and, between a cemetery and the railroad tracks, a driveway that led to the Emanuel Tire Company. Mostly open to the sky, it was laid out something like a lumberyard, and Norman Emanuel was off to one side, sitting in his office before a mural map. Hardly a word had passed between us before he sat me down opposite and began to fulminate about officials of the state and the city, not to mention the county. "They haven't found anything that I've done right, but the things I've been doing, they're eliminating that," he said. He was a big beefy dark-haired handsome tan-faced man with the build of a linebacker. He did not look urban, there in the middle of the middle of the city. He looked farm. Direct as he was, he was not always easy to understand. "Burl" equalled "barrel," as in "burl stacking"—the conventional way to stack tires. The form of water that drives turbines was "stame." He wore rubber boots, and his overalls were blue. His shirt was composed of rectangular checks of red, yellow, and black. On the forehead of his green-visored cap was the name of a company in North Carolina that had shown interest in burning Emanuel tire shreds to power machines that chip wood.

"We collect three million tires a year," Emanuel continued. "We'd be up to six or eight million now, but the state, they've cut my growth terribly."

It was growth that began in the nineteen-fifties, when he was nineteen years old and, while staying with a relative, found a job in a Baltimore Chevrolet plant. He was from Red Springs, in Robeson County, on the North Carolina coastal plain, where he grew up farming corn, cotton, wheat, and soybeans. In the Chevrolet cafeteria, he overheard a man saying that he had built a house on money he made collecting used tires and selling them for retreads. Norman Emanuel straightaway went to a service station and left with eight old tires. He sold three for three dollars apiece, and the Emanuel Tire Company had shown its first profit. Then he picked up thirty-one more. He sold thirty, and he never looked back.

To his eleven acres in Baltimore he brings tires from Florida, Georgia, South Carolina, North Carolina, Kentucky, Oklahoma, Virginia, West Virginia, Delaware, Pennsylvania, New Jersey, New York, and, of course, Maryland—each tire for a fee. "In 1978, when landfilling was phasing out, I knew I'd have to start making changes," he said. "I was the second person in the United States to have a tire shredder—after Pacific Energy, in Oregon. For a while, I landfilled the shreds."

Outside the office, a shredder was shredding. It was a squarish machine about twelve feet high with a couple of steel ladders and catwalks. Emanuel said, "Go ahead, go up and have a look." Tires were riding a conveyor to the top, and then falling into a hopperlike chamber whose bottom was a pair of rollers with steel teeth. Like the wringer on an old clothes washer, the rollers rolled toward each other, and when a tire fell on them it got caught in the crease. Slowly, quietly, the tire torqued, twisted, writhed—

like a snake caught up in a combine, attacked by the steel teeth, squeezed, folded, crushed, chopped, in a few seconds torn to shreds. (At a tire-shredding operation near Sacramento, not long ago, an employee was shredded.) Emanuel Tire has fourteen shredders, which make two-inch chips and smaller grades, on down to a quarter of an inch. Steel belt wire, like fish bones, protruded from the chips. The most concentrated steel in a tire is in the beads—the two hoops of cable in the rim-touching sides. Emanuel picked up a truck tire, put it on his debeader, and sliced out a bead. The hoop's braided steel was an inch in diameter.

Up the street in another lot were a couple of acres of shredded tires—plains and hills of shredded tires, a terrain that felt underfoot like a well-filled waterbed. To achieve such resiliency, all tires still contain some natural rubber. A big orthopterous machine—its narrow discharge conveyors reaching out like antennas—was chewing chopped tires and spewing product in three directions, forming conical mounds: chips fell to the left, steel forward, crumbs to the right. The chips were one-inch bits of tire. In a couple of days, the machine had piled up thirty tons of steel. Gesturing toward a modest mound of crumbs—a rubber drumlin not much higher than our heads—Emanuel said it represented ten thousand tires. It consisted of quarter-inch bits that felt in the hand like granola.

Emanuel's business has evolved so far away from landfills that nowadays, on principle, he said, he would sell shreds at a loss, if he had to, rather than put them in the ground. Over time, he has developed a roster of customers that is as varied as it is far-flung. He is reluctant to reveal who and where they are, but he will say that some of them are as far away from Baltimore as are St. Louis, Indianapolis, and Chicago. In some instances, he is more specific. He let it drop that the University of Virginia wanted forty tons of quarter-inch material for playing surfaces. For more than a decade, a rubber company in Trenton, New Jersey, had been making boots and gloves from shredded Emanuel tires. A good deal of crumb rubber goes for something he calls "reclaim," accenting the first syllable: running tracks, rubberized asphalt, railroad crossings.

In 1982, he began shipping shredded rubber to Spring Grove, Pennsylvania, for use as boiler fuel at a paper mill. Other paper mills followed, and now about a third of Emanuel's product "goes to burn for energy." One automobile tire, burning, will release about two hundred and fifty thousand British thermal units of energy—enough to heat fourteen hundred pounds of ice water to a boil. A tire contains considerably more energy than an equivalent weight of bituminous coal. United States paper mills, cement plants, and five hundred power plants currently burn bituminous coal. According to the California Integrated Waste Management Board, tires produce less ash and contain less sulphur than many commonly used types of coal, and with "no significant differences in emissions."

It has crossed Norman Emanuel's mind that he could keep the rubber he shreds and make use of it himself. He dreams sometimes of his own 1.5-megawatt power plant, and also of his own vegetable cannery, using "tires as fuel to make that stame." He says, "I see now that I could be almost self-sufficient."

He has in his stockpiles at any given time, in addition to shredded material, more than five hundred thousand tires graded to be sold for use on the road. Of the three million discarded tires that he annually collects, about seven hundred and fifty thousand are in good to excellent condition. One of his warehouses was half again as large as a football field. It was filled with tires that, by and large, were not burl stacked, one upon another, but densely laced, cross-bedded, adroitly assembled in converging angles by a method he called windrowing. The great room was as clean and tidy as a yarn shop.

"I hate a mess," he said. "I hate dirt."

On an amazing percentage of the inventory the treads were so high that the tires seemed new. He exports them all over the world. He has sent as many as a hundred thousand tires a year to Russia.

"Russia's a good market but you can't get no money."

Trade is brisk right there on Bentalou, where Baltimore bluebloods often cluster.

"People with Mercedes, people with Jaguars come here to buy tires."

His tall slender wife, Dafene, who is also from Robeson County, North Carolina, runs the office. She tries to keep up with the proliferating regulations that inhibit and threaten their business, and she appears to be a good deal cooler than he. A new state law limits them to fifteen thousand cubic feet of inventory, or about five truckloads of shredded material—the practical equivalent of nothing in a nation that throws away two hundred and fifty million tires a year and has about as many Norman Emanuels as congressmen from Alaska. Constricting regulations are what caused him to say, "They haven't found anything that I've done right, but the things I've been doing, they're eliminating that." He likes to let tire chips sit in weather for two to three years, so that oxidation will remove protruding steel—a process too passive to survive regulation. To date, he and Dafene have paid three hundred thousand dollars in legal fees in their effort to come to terms with the state. "The thing is simple: What can you do with tires? Landfill them or shred them. Why does the state want it gone from the face of the earth?" he asks, evidently asserting that the state wants the tires and the shreds to vanish but is not practically considering how that might happen. He grumbles that Texas and North Carolina are the only states that don't create problems for people who collect tires. He summarizes Maryland as follows: "The state says you've got to take tires to an approved place, but there's no place they approve. The State of Maryland, they stuff all their stuff into other states they can." He continues, "Everybody in this country is worried about a vote instead of doing what's right. They've forgot the difference between right and wrong. When I'm dead, everybody will know that I made a difference in solving this tire problem. I'll make it happen. You only live once in your life."

Aerial crop dusters use burning tires as wind socks. To attract fish, tires are piled in oceans as artificial reefs. Tires are amassed around harbors as porous breakwaters. In Guilford, Connecticut, Sally Richards grows mussels on tires. Tires are used on dairy farms to cover the tarps that cover silage. They stabilize the shoulders of highways, the slopes of drainage canals. They are set up as crash barriers, dock bumpers, fences, and playground tunnels and swings. At Churchill Downs, the paving blocks of the paddock are made of scrap tires. Used tires are used to fashion silent stairs. They weigh down ocean dragnets. They become airplane shock absorbers. They become sandals. Crumbled and granulated tires become mud flaps, hockey pucks, running tracks, carpet padding, and office-floor anti-fatigue mats. Australians make crumb rubber by freezing and then crushing tire chips. Japanese have laid railroad track on crumbled tires. Dirt racetracks seeded with crumbled tires are easier on horses. Crumbled tires added to soil will increase porosity and allow more oxygen to reach down to grass roots. Twelve thousand crumbled tires will treat one football field. In Colorado, corn was planted in soil that had been laced with crumbled tires. The corn developed large, strong roots. A mighty windstorm came and went, and the tire-treated field was the only corn left standing in that part of Colorado. All such uses, though, as imaginative and practical as they may be, draw down such a small fraction of the tires annually piled as scrap that while they address the problem they essentially do not affect it.

Retreads don't help much, either, in holding down the national pile, although Air Force One lands on retreads, the jets of the Blue Angels land on retreads, and when General H. Norman Schwarzkopf flew to the Gulf War he touched down on retreads. Almost all commercial airliners roll on retreaded tires. Most buses—including school buses—and most taxis are on retreads, and so are ten thousand Frito-Lay trucks and thirty-six thousand U.P.S. trucks. A company sensitive to costs per mile will retread its casings three times. A retread is in no way inferior to a new tire, but new tires are affordable, and the retreaded passenger tire has descended to the status of a clip-on tie. Not long ago, twenty-four million passenger tires were retreaded every year, but the number has declined nearly seventy per cent, swelling the volume of discards. Pilot plants have been erected to decompose tires through pyrolysis (destructive distillation, thermal degradation) in an attempt to recycle some of the fifteen million barrels of oil that are thrown away in tires in the United States each year. The process has not shown a profit. Tire chips go into rubber-modified asphalt concrete. RUMAC, as it is known, absorbs more heat than other surfaces do, gets rid of ice and snow, reduces glare, and makes a quiet road, a resilient road, a deformation-resistant road. A mile of RUMAC thirty-six feet wide and three inches thick uses sixteen thousand tires. The road lasts twice as long as ordinary asphalt. But ordinary asphalt is recycled, and that is hard to do if there is rubber in it. Few miles of American road are RUMAC.

When Jack Waggoner, of Sacramento, first wrote to me about the great tire pile of California, he mentioned that all the scrap tires now strewn about the American landscape would make a stack a hundred and forty-two thousand miles high. If you want to get rid of something like that, you don't try to do it by making lacrosse balls. The technological need is for consumption of old whole tires in a major useful way, and that, he said, was now going on at the big pile. Waggoner is an easygoing, ocean-fishing man in his fifties who has been in some aspect of the tire business all his adult life. In 1957, he was working in a Flying A service station in Lodi, near Stockton, when a customer said to him, "You do a hell of a job washing windshields. Come to work for me." The customer was impressive. Suit, tie, vest, hat, furled umbrella, he "looked like he should be calling on heads of state," but he was actually the sales manager of Super Mold, the largest manufacturer of tire-retreading machinery in the world. For years, Waggoner's territory included Japan, the Philippines, Indonesia, Ceylon, and islands of the South Pacific. He was "real heavy into Vietnam," where eight hundred truck tires were retreaded every day. Eventually, he started his own company, and when the retread business declined he augmented sales by distributing shredders. Driving south on I-5 toward the big pile, he said, "Once you get rubber in your veins, you can never get it out." I asked him why he, a purveyor of shredding machines, was interested in whole-tire recycling. He said, "Because it's the right thing to do."

On a dirt road behind a truck stop, we soon came to a guardhouse and a platinum-haired security man in a black leather jacket with a huge silver star. Waggoner was grata. No cameras allowed. We made our way into the range. On the hilltop opposite the tires was an electric plant with two Standardkessel boilers and a fueling technology of German design—taller than it was broad, like a castle by the Neckar or the Rhine. From the bottom of the valley rose a moving conveyor at least four hundred feet long. Tires were riding upward, and we climbed five stories of steel steps to watch them arrive. Producing stame, the structure was now and again fogged by its own swirling cloud, which blew off and revealed the creased hills. At the top of the conveyor was a carrousel that accepted the tires, carried them around, and watched them with electric eyes. When air-lock chambers were ready to receive them, fingers of steel came up through the carrousel and shoved them to one side. They went into the air-lock chambers, and then fell to a reciprocating grate—a nickel-chromium stoker grate—which looked something like a stairway, with accordion steps that contracted and expanded and advanced the tire toward the core of conflagration. You could watch this through a window, two inches in diameter. Scarcely had a new tire landed on the grate when—count one, count two—it burst into wild flame, at upward of twenty-five hundred degrees. At the far side of the fire chamber, where the fuel compacted and the heat was most intense, a peephole looked in at the climax of the burning. What appeared there resembled the cliff-like snout of a glacier, white in a bath of auroran red, with white particulate flying like snow, and lumps and bumps and moguls.

The plant was supplying enough power to Pacific Gas & Electric to fulfill the daily requirements of fifteen thousand homes. Among dedicated waste-to-energy fuels, tires have two to three times as many B.T.U.s as municipal solid waste, refuse-derived fuel, or biomass. Generally operating around the clock, the plant was burning seventeen thousand tires a day. It burns five million tires a year.

Filbin the Tire Jockey—having been paid, say, an average of a quarter of a dollar for collecting each of the many millions of tires he had stored here—was now selling them for slightly more to the energy company that owned the plant. Doug Tomison, the plant manager, mentioned "a royalty arrangement on a sliding scale," and the scale had to do with how many million tires were in the great pile. Tomison's rough estimate came in one digit. Tomison was a young dark-haired man on crutches. All in four weeks, he had hit a school bus with his motorcycle, a bee had stung him on the motorcycle, and a cow had kicked him off it, too. But that level of misfortune was painless compared with the kicking he was getting from the tire jockey. "He's killing us," Tomison said. "We're making a profit and giving it to him." By burning whole tires, the company was avoiding a shredding cost of twenty-five dollars a ton, but not even that could turn the thing around. They were paying Filbin over a million dollars a year.

The Attorney General of California has shown professional interest in the tire pile. One of many considerations is that if a smoldering fire were to spread far through it a river of oil would go out of the hills and into the California Aqueduct. Los Angeles' femoral artery, the California Aqueduct is close by Interstate 5, a few thousand yards from the tires and three hundred feet below them. Looking across the valley, we could see in the rolling black dunes tiny figures moving. They were people, carrying tires. One tire at a time, the people were shifting tens of thousands of tires—by hand, the only way to do it—creating fire lanes to satisfy the government.

In the power-plant compound, the second-largest structure was the bag house, full of Gore-Tex bags hung up like balloons. They remove fine ash down to three microns. Burning tires emit nitrogen and sulphur oxides (known as Nox and Sox), carbon monoxide, particulate matter, hydrocarbons, arsenic, cadmium, chromium, lead, zinc, dioxins and furans, polycyclic aromatic hydrocarbons, polychlorinated biphenyls, and benzene. These pollutants are also emitted by coal. About seventy-five per cent of the ash is a rock-like slag of ferrous oxide, which falls into a hopper with a steel-belted thud and hardly requires a filter. A process called Thermal DeNox deals with nitrogen oxides. There is a limestone-slurry spray scrubber to remove sulphur. The fly ash is largely zinc, which is the major pollutant, and it is trapped in the Gore-Tex bags. Computers by the roomful operate the machines. The pollution-control equipment cost seven million dollars. Well over half of the Nox gets away. Of the Sox, two per cent escapes, as do smaller amounts of carbon monoxide.

As the limestone slurry reacts with the sulphur dioxide, gypsum results—as much as twelve tons a day. Gypsum can be used as a "soil amendment." Farmers buy it all. Zinc is recovered as zinc. The iron oxide, for the most part, is stored, looking for a customer, but some is sold as gravel for use in cement.

The country over-all would do well to burn whole tires in making cement. Flanking Interstate 5 near Redding— two hundred miles north of Filbin's pile—are a limestone quarry and a cement plant. Powdered limestone and shale are fed into a cylindrical precalcining furnace—a ten-story tower—up the side of which runs a chain-conveyor with steel hooks. From each hook hangs a tire. The tires enter from chutes about halfway up the tower, and, as they drop, flash in fire. The mixture of stone and burning tires moves on into a huge revolving drum that is slightly inclined from the horizontal, spins two times a minute, and extends more than two hundred yards. The Fahrenheit temperature rises within it to twenty-six hundred degrees. As the rock, revolving, roasts, the tires supply not only heat but also the iron oxide indispensable to cement. The ash residue of the tires becomes a part of the chemistry of the cement. The tires disappear absolutely. Their steel is completely oxidized. The heat causes the limestone's calcium carbonate and carbon dioxide to separate, leaving calcium oxide, or quicklime. Then quicklime reacts with silica and alumina (in the shale) to form calcium silicates and aluminates, which leave the kiln as clinker in pieces the size of eggs. The clinker is ground with gypsum, and that is cement. No ash, no slag. In Germany and Japan, about twenty per cent of the fuel for cement plants is whole tires. The kiln in Redding—at the Calaveras Cement Company—consumes more than two hundred tires an hour. It has a bag house and other state-of-the-art pollution-control equipment. California has eleven cement plants, ten of which are close to cities, where the tires are. Those eleven plants could consume all of the twenty million tires annually discarded in California and dispose of five million additional tires as well. California cement plants require thirty-four trillion B.T.U.s a year, and ninety per cent of that energy is supplied by coal. In words of the California Integrated Waste Management Board, "The cement manufacturing industry could use all of the waste tires generated in the state as well as the existing stockpiles. . . . From an energy perspective, use of tires as a supplemental fuel in cement kilns displaces fossil fuels and results in no wastes and no significant differences in emissions." A cement plant near Santa Cruz applied for a permit to use tires but gave up because of the cost of fighting environmentalists.

In 1989, Anne Evans was invited by Great Britain's Department of Trade and Industry to develop in England a dedicated waste-to-energy tire-burning power plant like the one in California. She was thirty-three years old then. While still in her twenties, she had started a tire export-import business that operated in many countries around the world, including England, and her profits were very large. Always—in a shifting, chronic manner—tires became overstocked or understocked in this place and that. What she did was move them from supply to demand, meanwhile watching currency fluctuations, which she rode like thermals. "If you work very hard at that and don't get a lot of sleep, and if you understand letters of credit, you do very well," she told me. "The idea is to close a deal within twenty-four hours. You make a good relationship with a freight forwarder, and your life gets very simple. Be honest. Do a good job. Don't be greedy. And you'll do well."

Her distributors were involved not only with new tires but with old ones, and the problem of how to dispose of the old ones was everywhere increasing. She remembers her grandfather saying, "He who figures out what to do with these tires is going to make a million"—her grandfather Tony DiGiandomenico, who started the family's Firestone dealership and retreading company in Middletown. Her father, Mario Salemi, had rubber in his veins, too. His parents, and Tony DiGiandomenico's mother, came from Melilli, near Syracuse, in Sicily, as did so many other citizens of Middletown that they built an exact copy of Melilli's ornate and gilded Church of San Sebastiano. To this day, almost anybody from Middletown can cash a personal check in Melilli. It may be a little easier if your name is DiGiandomenico. Anne, at twenty-two and with scarcely any more business training than any other recent product of Newton College of the Sacred Heart, was working in Washington for the National Republican Congressional Campaign

Committee when her father fell ill and she went home to take over the tires.

Through the early nineteen nineties, she commuted from Connecticut, where her husband is a real-estate broker, to Wolverhampton, in the West Midlands, where she established a company called Elm Energy & Recycling. Wolverhampton is twelve miles from Birmingham. The plant occupies six acres. Except for its exhaust stack, it is an unobtrusive ground-hugging structure, in which tires are not stockpiled but arrive instead in a continuous stream of lorries. Michelin, Pirelli, Goodyear, Dunlop—all the big tire companies operate their own retail stores in England. They pay the haulers, who, in turn, pay Elm. All their waste tires go to Wolverhampton. The plant is capable of producing twenty-five megawatts, but sells no more than twenty. The rest of the power is needed to run the anti-pollution equipment. The site was dedicated in a tent in ceremonies overhung by chandeliers and enriched by a cello. The pneumatic Michelin man was outside, the chairman of Pirelli was inside. The plant now receives about twenty-five per cent of all tires discarded in the United Kingdom.

"We are the cleanest power station in England," she told me when we talked in Connecticut. "We're green. We're the best thing since peanut butter." She was obviously undaunted by her discovery that, as she put it, "the English are not receptive to women." She said, "There might as well be a sign at Heathrow: 'If you are a woman doing business, go home.' "

She went on to say, "Energy is a good thing for tires. Landfilling should not happen. That's a total waste—of land, of material. But energy may be just another step in the evolution." She thinks that tires themselves will change. She imagines them somehow being made differently, so that the disposal problem will take care of itself. "Tires will change as cars change. Now they hold the shock. That may be put somewhere else. Tires may be different. A different material. Who knows what?" Meanwhile, she was much impressed by a research scientist for a German tire company who studied tires-to-energy and said, "Maybe we can take something out of the tire to make it easier to burn."

"The consumer has got to be willing to pay mandated disposal fees," she concluded. "It costs money to do it right. Every bit of material should be used to its fullest extent. A tire in its first life is a tire. It needs to be used for something further. Unless we do that, we're wasteful. The reality of life is that we can't afford to be wasteful anymore. Let's do something else with this material when we're finished with it, and we'll be in good shape in the next generation. That takes an industrial commitment. It's not a legislative matter. You can't legislate people to feel a certain way. It's got to be in them to say, 'We've got to do this as a society.' When governments raise tipping fees, illegal dumping rises. In England, when someone takes tires away for fifteen pence a tire and dumps them in a vacant lot, it is known as fly tipping. That is why there is a law in England called Duty of Care: you need a waste-management license; you have to know exactly what happens to your waste. The tire stores have to know."

"Do we have such a law?"

"Of course not."

Note: The description of the piled tires in Stanislaus County, California, dates from February, 1991. In September, 1999, when roughly seven million remained, lightning struck a loading platform among the tires and ignited a fire that burned for more than a month. In the words of Chris Thompson, a staff writer for the *East Bay Express*, "A column of obsidian smoke, the size of a small city, rose miles into the sky and blotted out the sun. It was a roiling, sulfurous, unctuous golem, beyond the control of those men who had set into motion the events that led to its appalling birth. Take the amount of oil spilled in the Exxon *Valdez* disaster, add another three million gallons, then set it on fire, and you begin to appreciate the scale of the Westley inferno."

RINARD

AT

MANHEIM

.

Most dealers don't need exotics on their lots. Some dealers specialize in exotics. The Manheim Exotic Auction is strictly wholesale—where dealers sell to other dealers. You're not going to see any Duesenbergs today, no Hudsons, no Singers, no Delahayes, no Cords. I did see a Boattail here once. The rear end comes to a point. But this is not an antique-auto show, it's a sale of modern, used exotic cars. Ferraris are exotics. Rolls-Royce. Porsche. Jaguar. Mercedes. BMW. Sprinkled among these will be true exotics, such as Excaliburs, Avantis, and AC Cobras. With thirty or forty thousand miles on them, they will sell for thirty or forty thousand dollars. Lotus is a true exotic, too. There'll be some Loti here. The Lamborghini Countach is the ultimate exotic.

[*Lamborghini Coon Tosh.*]

The Lamborghini Countach is noisy, uncomfortable, and hot; but it has gull-wing doors and looks like a spaceship, and there are those who must have it.

[*He mentions certain publishers.*]

A Lamborghini went through for ninety-five thousand

dollars the last time I was here. No sale. The owner wanted more. The owner-dealer stands by the auctioneer and can refuse a sale. A Rolls-Royce convertible goes through. Someone bids a hundred thousand dollars. No sale. A hundred thousand is not enough. I'm a scout here. A consultant. Officially, a designated buyer. Most times, I buy nothing. I represent Hype. A New Jersey dealer named Hype. Dealers from all over come to the Manheim Exotic Auction. It happens five or six times a year. They come from New York, Maryland, Connecticut, Delaware, Ohio, Virginia. They come in chartered planes and take limos from Lancaster Airport. They may be wearing leather jackets, but that only masks their money. They have places in the Bahamas. The last time I came to the Exotic, driving through here on the back roads I counted twenty-three buggies.

[*This is the front-porch country of the Pennsylvania Dutch. The country, too, of the Mennonites. A sign outside a high school says "Welcome, German Exchange Students." Frame houses lie in tight rows in the otherwise open landscape. The exotics, side by side, are lined up like the houses. The Manheim Exotic Auction—just down Route 72 from Ristenbatt's vacuum-cleaner service, Dutchland Motor Company, and the Smoke Haus Tavern—is in a fenced space as open as an airfield.*]

Rabbit convertibles are the low end of the exotic scale. You will see a few Rabbit convertibles here, but probably you won't see anything as modest as a BMW 325. It is known as an entry-level car. What you'll mainly see is the top end of each line. The Ferrari Testarossa and Ferrari F-40 are superexotics. I don't think there's an F-40 in this country. For us, the Testarossa is the ultimate exotic. Very habitable. The fastest car you can buy off a showroom floor at this time. It'll go a hundred and seventy-eight miles an hour. It has more room than a Countach. It's not as hot, not as uncomfortable, easier to get in and out. You have to be an athlete to get into a Countach.

[*He is my friend Rinard. Friend since high school. He carries the dealer's plastic card, knows more about this topic than most dealers do. He walks the exotic line.*]

White Lotus Esprit Turbo. Known as the paint scraper. Looks like one. Styled by Giugiaro. You can have it new for fifty-five thousand dollars. The question is: Can any four-cylinder be worth that much money?

Avanti. Basically a Studebaker with a big Chevrolet V-8 engine in it. What color would I call that? Rust. However, you don't say "rust" around a car lot. You don't use that word.

Porsche 928 S4. This is the ultimate exotic. Quiet. Incredibly smooth.

[*It has the headlights of a flounder. In repose, lying back, they look up at the sky.*]

It's the most civilized and most expensive of Porsches. Costs sixty-five thousand new. A hundred and fifty-five miles per hour. Before the Testarossa, it was the fastest you could buy.

E-Type Jaguar, with that great big 4.2 litre V-12 engine. Generally voted the most beautiful car ever designed.

[*In front view, a cross between a cat and a chipmunk.*]

Porsche 911 twin-turbo slant-nose. A sports-car enthusiast's sports car. You pay twenty thousand dollars more for the slant-nose.

Maserati Biturbo. Extremely fast in a straight line. What does that mean? It means you may lower your opinion when you turn the wheel.

Ferrari 308. This is your basic exotic. Ninety-some per cent of Ferraris are red, don't ask me why.

BMW 325. Call me a liar, there's one here—an entry-level car. I can put you in this for thirteen thousand dollars. It's a mere bag of shells.

Toyota Supra. Things are getting worse. Well, you can sneak a couple of Supras in here. It's a nice car, but you're carrying around thirty-five hundred pounds.

That Rabbit convertible, with the orphan tire, is high in the miles; this Audi 5000, without turbo, is a little weak in the knees.

Cadillac Allanté. Two years old, costs fifty-seven thousand new. This is Cadillac's answer to all the other cars around here, and it's not a very good answer. It's under-powered. Two seats. Detroit iron. Nice, but compare it with a Jaguar XJS, which is quieter, smoother, handles better, is faster, and costs twenty thousand dollars less. Allanté, with its *accent aigu*, is a word that means nothing in any known language, like Exxon and Häagen-Dazs.

[*Rinard stations himself in midstream as cars begin to flow toward the auction shed. Those that attract his attention he follows in. They could be sheep. They could be tobacco leaves. Above each auctioneer are six lights. Green: Sound. Yellow: Listen. Red: Caution. Blue: Title Attached. Orange: No air. Magenta: Diesel. Old auctioneer in ten-gallon hat. Young auctioneer in white shirt, dark tie, dark-blue suit. Handkerchief in his left hand over the mike. In his right hand, a length of rubber hose. "Heydababababababeedabeedabee-dabodabupbupbedupup thirty-one five, thirty-one five, bup-upabupup, thirty-one five." Whap with the rubber. "Sir, you bought a car." Sir has bought a Jaguar XJ6.*]

The Lotus is coming up. Ninety-two hundred miles. It cost fifty-five thousand new.

[*"Beedabodabupbupbedupup, thirty-three five." Auc-tioneer turns head for signal from owner. "No sale." Avanti, thirty-six thousand miles, fifteen five, no sale. Jaguar XJ6, lovely hemlock green, fifteen five, no sale. Mercedes SEL.*

Fifty-two thousand once, fifty-two thousand twice. Whap. No sale. Mercedes 560 SEC. Fifty-six thousand three hundred dollars. No sale.]

In the Exotic, half the cars are not sold. The guy who wants the car has got to be here. Dealers crowd around the cars they want. The biggest crowd today will collect around the Porsche 928 S4.

[*With the flounder eyes. The dealers swarm like fans around a goalpost. They open doors. Look under the hood. "Bedupbedupup. Fifty-two five. No sale." Cadillac Allanté, under nine thousand miles, twenty-eight thousand dollars bid. Sold. Rolls-Royce, three years old, thirty-four thousand miles. Cost a hundred and ten thousand dollars new. Bedupup. Whap. Fifty-four thousand five hundred dollars. "Buddy, you bought a car."*]

That's what I call depreciation.

[*Maserati Biturbo on the block. Buzzer sounds. "Bupupabeedup. Roll the car." Each car has three minutes before the crowd. Its fate is resolved after it is gone.*]

Here is that E-Type Jaguar. It's the ultimate exotic.

[*Not today. No sale.*]

This is an '81 DeLorean. Relax, I know where to get you parts. Stainless steel—the DeLorean basic color. You can have any color you want as long as it's stainless. It has a basic Peugeot engine, not outstanding but very good. It has an X-frame—very expensive. It's supposed to give you better handling. You'd need to bid fifteen thousand dollars.

[*As the crowd paws it over, the doors of the DeLorean rise like the wings of a raptor.*]

You can see why he went bankrupt. It's a nice car, but where's the market? How many Jay Gatsbys are there in the world?

[John McPhee]

TRAVELS

OF THE

ROCK

.

Plymouth Rock is a glacial erratic at rest in exotic terrane. When Mayflower, an English merchant ship, approached the rock, in 1620, the rock, like the ship, had recently been somewhere else. Heaven knew where. Some geologists have said that the rock is Laurentian granite, from north of the St. Lawrence River (Loring, 1920). Most American geologists have preferred a provenance closer to home: Cape Ann, for example, north of Boston (Carnegie Institution, 1923); or the region of Cohasset, south of Boston (Shimer, 1951); or even the bed of Plymouth Bay (Mather, 1952). Wherever the boulder came from, it was many times larger in 1620 than it is today.

It was also in one piece. In 1774, the rock was split in two, horizontally, like a bagel. There were those who feared and those who hoped that the break in the rock portended an irreversible rupture between England and the American colonies. If so, the lower half was the Tory half, for it stayed behind, while the upper part was moved from the harborside to Liberty Pole Square for the specific purpose of stirring up lust for independence. Scarce was independence half a century old when a new portentous split occurred, in the upper, American, rock. It broke, vertically, into two principal parts, shedding fragments to the side. Eventually, the two halves of the upper part were rejoined by common mortar, containing glacial pebbles from countless sources, and the rock as a whole was reconstructed. The upper part was returned to the waterfront, where a thick filling of mortar was slathered on the lower part, and Plymouth Rock—with its great sutured gash appearing like a surgical scar—was reassembled so that it would be, to whatever extent remained possible, a simulacrum of the landmark that was there in 1620.

In the course of the twentieth century, the mortar did not hold. Pebbles fell out. Chunks. Despite a canopy over the rock (McKim, Mead & White, 1921), water got into the great crack, froze, and wedged against the bonding force with pressures as high as two thousand pounds per square inch. The rock could not stay whole, and on August 7, 1989, in an item disseminated by the Associated Press, the Massachusetts Department of Environmental Management announced that the oldest symbol of the New World was in dire need of a mason.

In the British merchant marine, Mayflowers were numerous. The one that approached the landmark in Plymouth Bay that December was twelve or so years old, and had, for the most part, carried wine to England from Bordeaux. Her new assignment was equally commercial. When she sailed from Devon, she was under instructions to go to the mouth of the Hudson River, where her passengers, under a seven-year contract with investors in London, would warehouse timber, furs, and fish. She was meant to land on New York rock, but she missed. After a crossing of nine stormy weeks, she came upon Cape Cod. She dropped anchor in the cape's sheltered bay and spent a month there while a number of passengers, including William Bradford, went ashore to reconnoitre the cape's resources. In the woods one day, Bradford noticed a sapling bent over like a dancer touching the ground. Acorns were strewn beneath the sapling. Bradford moved close, too close, and "it gave a sudden jerk up, and he was immediately caught by the leg" (Mourt, 1622). The noose that caught him was state of the art by English standards, and so was the rope. In their searches the explorers found stored corn in buried baskets, which they took for their own use. They opened the grave of a child. "About the legs and other parts of it was bound strings and bracelets of fine white beads; there was also by it a little bow, about three quarters long, and some other odd knacks. We brought sundry of the prettiest things away with us, and covered the corpse up again." Before the sun had set four times, "arrows came flying amongst us."

In a small sloop, a scouting party sailed west, into a gale that broke the boat's rudder and shattered the mast. Nonetheless, they found what is now Plymouth Harbor, climbed to the high defendable ground behind it, discovered a sweet brook and deserted fields. This was not the "rock-bound coast" that poetry and fiction would claim it to be. The shore was sandy. It was a beach. It was a long strand of wave-sorted till with almost no rocks of any size. A most notable exception was a big boulder of more than two hundred tons, alternately washed and abandoned by the cycle of the tides—a rock so prominently alone that from across water it would have looked like a house.

Bradford, Carver, Standish, Winslow, Howland, and the others—the exploring party—sailed back to Cape Cod to inform the Mayflower company that they had chosen a site for the plantation. They learned that Bradford's wife, Dorothy, had gone over the side of the ship and had drowned. She was one of four who died before the ship reached Plymouth. To get ashore on the cape, the people had to wade in several feet of water. Temperatures were often below the freeze point. Rain and spray formed ice on their clothing. Most of the children as well as the adults had colds, coughs, pneumonic symptoms that plunged into scurvy. On that gray water under gray sky—under wind and through snow—the land around them must have seemed less than promised. There had been a hundred and two passengers in all. One by one, across the next few months, forty-seven more would die.

A few days before Christmas, the ship entered Plymouth Harbor and approached the site near the mouth of the brook, the landmark rock below the foot of the hill. Most of the people lived on the ship until the end of March, routinely coming and going to trap or hunt or work on the initial construction. The brook, entering the bay, had cut a channel in the otherwise shallow water. The channel turned north, paralleled the shore, and ran close to the seaward side of the great rock. For two hundred years, oceangoing vessels would use this channel.

After the theory of continental glaciation was developed and accepted, in the nineteenth century, geologists reviewing the story of Plymouth took pleasure in pointing out that the rock had travelled, too: "The Pilgrims' Rock is . . . itself an older pilgrim than those who landed on it" (Adams, 1882). "Plymouth Rock is a bowlder from the vicinity of Boston, having accomplished its pilgrimage long before the departure of the Mayflower from Holland"

(Wright, 1905, "The Ice Age in North America and Its Bearings Upon the Antiquity of Man").

A headline in the New York *Times* of October 25, 1923, said:

PLYMOUTH ROCK CANADIAN

What followed was a summary of confident assertions emanating from the Geology Department of the University of Rochester. The news caused the Acting Governor of Massachusetts to schedule hearings. The news caused Charles E. Munroe, the chairman of the Committee on Explosives Investigations, of the National Research Council, in Washington, to write a "PERSONAL—Confidential" letter to Robert Lincoln O'Brien, the editor of the Boston *Herald*, seeking his assistance in developing an investigation that would yield "more complete knowledge of the rock" and, fortuitously, "trace its origin to some other locality than Canada, thus greatly relieving the minds and assuaging the feelings of many, not only within New England but without."

What Munroe wanted was a piece of the rock. He wanted to place a hand specimen in the hand of Henry S. Washington, petrologist, geologist, geochemist, of the Carnegie Institution's Geophysical Laboratory. O'Brien, in turn, put the request to Arthur Lord, the president of the Pilgrim Society, in Plymouth. Lord replied that the rock had *been* studied by geologists and identified as syenite. Syenite? said Munroe to Henry Washington. Where could that be from? Montreal, said Henry Washington. Or half a dozen places in Ontario. He also identified possible sources in Vermont, New Hampshire, Maine, and Massachusetts, including Cape Ann. Cape Ann was the likeliest of this lot. Large boulders glacially transported are seldom moved very far.

When the theory of plate tectonics congealed, in the late nineteen-sixties, it opened corridors of thought that have led to a complete revision of the geologic history of New England, where, it now appears, there is enough alien rock to effect the total detonation of the late chairman of the Committee on Explosives Investigations if he were here to hear about it. The short travels of glacial boulders are ignored by these new insights. In present theory, New England's very bedrock has come from overseas.

In Reston, Virginia, not long ago, at the headquarters of the United States Geological Survey, E-an Zen invited me to have a look at a snapshot taken from a space shuttle a hundred and sixty miles above Plymouth. The picture was nine inches high and eighteen wide. It had been made with a Large Format Camera. As with the old view cameras from the era of Mathew Brady, the negative was as large as the print. With a casual glance, you could see at once the region the picture covered. You could see Lake George, in the Adirondacks. You could see Vermont lakes, the Connecticut River, Narragansett Bay, and Cape Cod. But the picture was of such small scale—from eight hundred and forty-five thousand feet—that most of it seemed to the unaided eye a swirl of white patches in varying abstracts of gray. It covered, after all, at least twenty-four thousand square miles. Zen handed me a Hastings Triplet, a ten-power lens that geologists hold close to outcrops and specimens in order to study crystals. He put his finger on the edge of Massachusetts Bay, and said, "Look there." I leaned close to the photograph, as if it were a rock, and saw stripes at the head of a runway at Logan Airport. Moving the lens down the coast, I saw the breakwater in Plymouth Harbor. I saw Town Brook, Town Wharf, State Pier, and Coles Hill. I did not see Plymouth Rock, because of the canopy above it. On the shore of a Vermont lake I saw a small outcrop called White

Rock, which I knew from childhood. Zen also had a picture that reached from Montreal to the Maine coast. I saw the house of a friend of mine on Mount Desert Island. I saw a fourteen-acre island in Lake Winnipesaukee, where I fish for chain pickerel in the fall. I saw smoke drifting away from the weather station at the summit of Mt. Washington.

After I put down the hand lens and leaned back, Zen asked if I could discern in the unmagnified pictures variations in texture from one area to another. I said I could. The country east of the Penobscot River, for example, differed from the country to the west as, say, burlap differs from tweed. Most variations were more subtle. On those pictures, from that altitude, the differences were no greater than the differences that sometimes occur on the surface of a calm lake. But the differences were there. New England appeared to consist of several swaths, as much as a hundred miles wide and more or less parallel to the seacoast. Zen was sporting a pleased grin. The large-format photographs seemed to illustrate conclusions he had reached from paleomagnetic, petrologic, structural, and seismic data interpreted in the light of plate tectonics, and in no way refuted by paleontology. Placing a finger on each side of the Penobscot River, he said those differing textural bands were exotic terranes.

As plate theorists reconstruct plate motions backward through time, they see landmasses now represented by Europe and Africa closing together with North America during the Paleozoic Era. These were the assembling motions that produced the great continent Pangaea. Much more recently, western Pangaea split apart to form the Atlantic Ocean, which is young, and is widening still. The ocean that was closed out in the making of Pangaea—the older ocean, the ancestral Atlantic, which used to be approximately where the Atlantic is now—is commonly called Iapetus, since Iapetus was the father of Atlas, and plate theorists, in studied humility, thus record their debt to mythology. The collision, as Zen and others see it in the rock they study and the data they otherwise collect, was not a simple suture of the two great sides. There were islands involved, and island arcs— Madagascars, New Zealands, Sumatras, Japans. "They were large islands in an ocean of unspecified size," he said. "Islands like Newfoundland." Some of them may have amalgamated while still standing off in the ocean. Some not. In one way or another, they were eventually laminated into Pangaea, and slathered like mortar between the huger bodies of rock.

A couple of hundred million years later, as the Atlantic opened, bits and pieces of original America stuck to Europe and rode east. The Outer Hebrides, for example, are said to derive from the northern North American continental core.

HEBRIDES CANADIAN

The converse was true as well. Stuck to North America, fragments of Europe stayed behind. Baltimore, for example. Nova Scotia. A piece of Staten Island.

The part of Massachusetts that includes Plymouth and Boston is now understood to derive from overseas. If from Europe, part of New England could be part of Old England, a New Old England in an Old New England or an Old Old England in a New New England. The Mayflower people landed where they left.

Around eight one morning in mid-November of 1989, Paul Choquette, of South Dartmouth, Massachusetts, who had been selected only three days earlier as Mason to the

Rock, arrived in Plymouth under considerable pressure to get the repair work done well before Thanksgiving, which was eight days away. He showed up in a U-Haul truck with Nebraska license plates and this message emblazoned on the sides: "ONE-WAY & LOCAL/ADVENTURE IN MOVING." Choquette was a trim man in his forties, with green eyes, dense brown hair, a loose, lean frame, and the serious look of a concentrating golfer. There was, as well, resemblance to a golfer in his roomily draped wine-red sweater, in his striped collar hanging free, less so in his bluejeans and his white running shoes. He had with him his entire family and then some. He had Jonathan, Jennifer, Elizabeth, and Tim—his children, twelve to twenty-one. He had his brother-in-law, Richard Langlois, and Richard's six-year-old, Ian, who said, "Why is this important? There's no such thing as Pilgrims."

Mark Cullinan, the chief engineer of the Department of Environmental Management, remarked that Choquette's task would be something like taking the tonsils out of the President of the United States—a relatively minor operation that nonetheless required someone of more than ordinary skill in the art. Moreover, the work would be accomplished with a lot of people watching: the public and the media, not to mention Paul Botelho, Cullinan's assistant chief engineer; Ruth Teixeira, the Region 1 regional engineer; Ronald Hirschfeld, a geotechnical consulting engineer; Chris Green, a landscape architect of the Office of Cultural and Historic Landscapes of the Department of Environmental Management; Peter O'Neil, the departmental press secretary; Shelley Beeby, the deputy commissioner of communications; and Donald Matinzi, of Plymouth, the park supervisor.

This was a day of chilling, intermittently heavy rain, and no one was sorry to be standing inside the McKim,

Mead & White portico, which is locally known as the cage. It's a bit like a Bernese bear pit. Granite walls enclose the rock on three sides. The fourth side, through iron grillwork, is open to the sea. The entablature is supported on twelve tall columns, and is six feet thick, or thick enough to block rain. Under it, visitors stand behind iron railings looking down at the rock on its patch of beach.

The rock has become fairly round and has a diameter varying from five and a half to six and a half feet. Early in the eighteenth century, it was measured for purposes of a town plat, with the resulting description that the "Grate Rock yt lyeth below Ye sd Way from ye stone at ye foot of The hill neare the Southerly Corner of John Ward's land is :30: foot in width" (Plymouth Records, 1715–16). What you see now weighs only four tons. The lower, buried part is larger. Spring tides climb into the cage and far up the rock. Nor'easters drive seas against it as well. When trucks go by on Water Street, the rock shakes.

The rock is filled with xenoliths—alien and black. They are stones, cobbles, hunks of older rock that fell into the larger mass while it was still molten or, if cooler than that, sufficiently yielding to be receptive. The xenoliths are like raisins in a matrix of bread. The rock is crisscrossed with very narrow, very straight veins of quartz. At some point in the nineteenth century, it cracked along one or two of these veins.

On the seaward side, the old repair was in particular need of attention. The national treasure looked sorry indeed, like twice-broken crockery. After the news of its condition went out on the A.P., epoxy-makers all over the country offered their expertise free of charge. But Cullinan decided that high-strength epoxy was too much of a high-tech solution. To get rid of it, if that should ever be necessary, you would have to destroy rock.

Mortars can be mixed that look like stone. In other words, despite the fact that the great crack was as wide as a python, an effort could be made to fool the public into thinking it wasn't there. Cullinan rejected that idea, too. The remaining choice—other than leaving the rock alone —was to chip out the old mortar and replace it.

Choquette climbed down into the cage with so many others that they did suggest a surgical team. He had his duckbill chisel, his cold chisels, his brick hammer, his five-pound hammer, his three-pound hammer, his paint-brushes, his wire brushes, his cord, his trowels, his wrenches, and his two sons. His brother-in-law stacked three planks against the iron grillwork on the seaward side and wrapped a rubber sheet around them in anticipation of the rising tide. It was a day of full moon.

Choquette went at the crack with a chisel. Tap. Tap. Ta-tap-tap-tump. He said, "Listen to that void!" Bits of mortar flew away. The opening widened. After a couple of hundred taps, he reached in and pulled seaweed out of Plymouth Rock. It was dry, and looked like twigs and straw. It came out of the interior like mattress stuffing.

He said the old mortar was very hard—"a lot of Port-land and not much lime." In replacing it, he would use four parts pulverized stone and four parts aggregate with one part lime (for plasticity). He would clean the crack with Detergent 600. He would put his new mortar in and, twenty minutes later, wash it with a hose and brush it. This would get rid of lime that tends to come to the surface. It would make the mortar darker, and also cause it to blend better into the pores of the rock.

To show to anyone who might be interested, he had a yogurt cup full of the pulverized stone. It came from a quarry in Acushnet, he said. Acushnet, Massachusetts, next to New Bedford, sits on hundreds of feet of long-transport glacial till. It is probable that the shards of rock going into Choquette's mortar came from three or four New England states and much of eastern Canada, and, in turn, from almost any Old World country south of Lapland. If a corner of the Old World was missing in the pulverized till, it might well be represented among the small angular stones that Choquette had brought from his own property, in South Dartmouth, to match the aggregate in the existing mortar. Steadily tapping, he continued to clean out the rock.

From above, someone in the gathering crowd asked him why he was attracted to this sort of specialty.

He said, "It intrigues me. Everything today is fast track. You know—you work it up and say, 'Where's the check?'"

"Are you ready for the Liberty Bell?"

"If you give me a shot at it, I'll try." Tap. Ta-tap-taptump. "This rock is already eighty per cent gone. Even if we can preserve ten per cent of it, we should preserve it. What matters is what it means."

The Department of Environmental Management had sought an expert mason who had experience with historic masonry. The Historic Commissions of five states were asked for recommendations. This produced a short list of eight masons, including the restorer of Belvedere Castle, in Manhattan's Central Park, and the restorer of Austin Block, in the Charlestown section of Boston—a three-story granite building made of rock from an island in Boston Harbor. Seven years earlier, Choquette had reached his decision that there had to be more in masonry than trowelling together new buildings. Venturing into restoration as often as he got a chance, he had done the exterior of the Academy of Music Theatre, in Northampton, the exterior of a church in New Bedford, and various lithic antiquities on Nantucket. As masons were evaluated for the Plymouth assignment, they were asked in formal interviews what approach they would take to the problem—to say in detail just how they would think through and plan the work. Among the candidates was one who replied, "You wanta me to fix the crack, right? I do a good job. It take an hour." The finalists were Steve Striebel, of Gill, Massachusetts, and Paul Choquette. The job then went to bids. Striebel's bid was a hundred times as high as Choquette's. So Choquette got the job. He bid a dollar.

In November and December of 1620, Mayflower people landed (and slept) in half a dozen places before reaching and settling in Plymouth. In the two contemporary accounts of the Plymouth landings—the several landings of the exploring sloop, and the arrival of the ship itself—nowhere is it mentioned, or obliquely suggested, that anyone set foot on a rock (Mourt, 1622; Bradford, 1630–50). Yet by 1820 the rock was set in the diadem of the republic. Daniel Webster, as the principal speaker on Forefathers' Day, on the two-hundredth anniversary of the Plymouth settlement, said, "Beneath us is the rock on which New England received the feet of the Pilgrims." He continued for an hour, his eloquent images provoking tears, and no one seemed to doubt him. The media had long since accepted the story. "The Federalists toasted their ancestors with the hope that the empire which sprung from their labors be as permanent as the rock of their landing" (*Colombian Sentinel*, December 22, 1798). And when Plymouth's first official history was published it said, "The identical rock, on which the sea-wearied Pilgrims first leaped . . . has never been a subject of doubtful designation" (Thacher, 1832). Foreign journalists covering the United States noted in conversations with Americans everywhere what "an object of veneration" the rock had become—a reverence that was growing in inverse proportion to the size of the rock itself. "I saw bits of it carefully preserved in several towns of the Union. . . . Here is a stone which the feet of a few outcasts pressed for an instant, and the stone becomes famous; it is treasured by a great nation; its very dust is shared as a relic" (Tocqueville, 1835).

Inevitably, a shrine was built to enshrine it—a tall four-legged canopy reaching back in time to Trajan and the baldachino and forward to the missile silo. The designer was Hammatt Billings, the illustrator of "Uncle Tom's Cabin," "Mother Goose," and "Little Women." It stood for fifty-three years before it was replaced by McKim, Mead & White. The rock that fitted into this ciborium not only had travelled across an ocean as bedrock and then an unknown distance as a glacial boulder but also had become remarkably mobile in Plymouth. When twenty yoke of oxen were brought to the site to move it, in 1774, pitonlike screws were put into it to assist the operation. The splitting occurred as if in a quarry, and the oxen went off with half a rock. On the Fourth of July, 1834, that upper half was moved several blocks, from the town square to the yard of Pilgrim Hall. In a two-wheeled cart, it was drawn through Plymouth as if it were the bull Ferdinand. It was escorted by the Plymouth Band, the Standish Guards, and half a dozen youths hauling behind them a model of the Mayflower. A story has come down from that parade to the effect that a pin came out of the bed of the cart, causing it to tilt, and—with the whole town of Plymouth looking on—the rock crashed to earth and broke into several pieces. Of the crisscrossing quartz veins in Plymouth Rock, each is a healed crack. The cracking and the healing could be associated with its original cooling (when its temperature got down to about a thousand degrees Fahrenheit), or with tectonic activity (anything from local faulting to pervasive plate motions) that heated it up. In either case, the quartz seams are planes of weakness—quarrymen call them sap streaks—and the break that Paul Choquette would one day be asked to fix followed such a vein. Since the story of the parade accident lacks convincing roots, it is probable that the rock's famous crack was made over years by rainwater, penetrating along a vein, freezing, wedging.

Meanwhile, the lower half of the rock remained at the waterfront, and actually served as a part of the surface of a commercial wharf, with iron-tired carts rolling over it filled with fish or lobsters, timber, coal. In the mud-traceried right-of-way, it bloomed like a plantar wart. It was a few feet from the front step of a grocery. When tourists came to see the rock, the grocer swept it clean, saying that he was "brushing off the cornerstone of the nation," and if anyone wanted a souvenir there was a hammer and chisel near the door. While Billings' canopy was under construction, the lower-half rock was hoisted up and placed to one side. As it sat there for some years exposed, it lost considerable weight. Large pieces were broken off and stolen. Some were rebroken into small pieces that were individually sold or, in one case, used as aggregate in making a concrete floor. A few large hunks went into a pickle barrel to weigh down corning beef. A piece that weighed four hundred pounds became a doorstep.

In 1867, when the lower half of the original rock was placed in its new setting, it did not fit. It was too long and thick for the display purposes the designer had in mind. So the rock was trimmed and planed. Its upper surface was lowered, as chips flew.

In 1880, the halves were reunited. The upper half was hauled downhill and set on top of the piece in the canopy. Together, the two parts were about as stable now as an egg resting on an egg. They were chinked firm by imported rocks of no established pedigree. Into the upper half the date 1620 was chiselled boldly.

At the time of the tercentenary, the Plymouth shoreline was reconfigured, and some thousands of tons of large broken rock were lined up as riprap on the once sandy beach. The old canopy was removed to make way for the new portico. As the national triolith was lifted by a crane, its repaired crack widened and the parts separated. The Obelisk Waterproofing Company, of New York City, was called in to waterproof the rock. This done, Plymouth Rock in its several parts was put on skids and hauled to a warehouse, where it remained until the portico was ready. In 1921, with mortar and trowel, the sculptor Cyrus Dallin reassembled the parts. His standing bronze figure of Chief Massasoit watched from Coles Hill, the high defendable ground above.

I am indebted to Julie Johnson, of Boston, who once studied Plymouth Rock for the Department of Environmental Management and whose specialty is historic preservation, for guiding me to a large part of this research, in the archives of Pilgrim Hall, in Plymouth.

The rock came to Plymouth about twenty thousand years ago. During the past couple of centuries, much of it has continued to travel, and some has recrossed the sea. A trimmed, squared hundred-pound piece long stood on a twenty-foot plinth in the courtyard of an inn at Immingham, in Lincolnshire, where, on the Humberside in 1607, the disaffected Puritans departed for Holland. There are pieces of Plymouth Rock at the Conoco refinery in Hull, Massachusetts. A piece of Plymouth Rock that weighs more than fifty pounds is in the Plymouth Congregational Church, on Schermerhorn Street, in Brooklyn. There is a piece of Plymouth Rock in Los Gatos, California. There is a piece of Plymouth Rock in the Nevada State Museum, in Carson City. In the Smithsonian Institution, in Washington, is a piece of Plymouth Rock about twenty-two inches long and of such craggy beauty that it could serve the art of *suiseki*, in which it would be called a distant-mountain stone. In the nineteen-twenties, the Antiquarian Society of Plymouth sold pieces of the rock as paperweights. There have been tie tacks, pendants, earrings, cufflinks made from Plymouth Rock. In 1954, a patriotic citizen sent President Eisenhower a piece of Plymouth Rock with the message "Now, Mr. President, if there are times when the going is hard and you may be discouraged, just take this little stone in your hand and . . ." Ike wrote back to thank him.

E-an Zen, who is approximately as exotic as the rock he studies, was born in Peking in 1928 and came to the United States when he was eighteen years old. Educated at Cornell and Harvard, he has worked primarily in the northern Appalachians. He seems to know every outcrop, contour, brook, and village of New England. Zen is wiry, spare, compact. It is not unimaginable that the term "rock-ribbed" was coined so that it would exist to describe him. He is the editor of the geologic map of Massachusetts (Zen, Goldsmith, Ratcliffe, Robinson, Stanley, 1983). Among his benchmark papers is one that is titled "Exotic Terranes in the New England Appalachians" (1983). When I saw him in Reston, he had recently written a guidebook for the International Geological Congress, laying out a field trip across the complete aggregation of terranes from Saratoga County, New York, through Vermont, New Hampshire, and Massachusetts to the coast of Rhode Island. He showed me the map the field trip followed. Rutland and Bennington, in Vermont, and Williamstown and Stockbridge, in Massachusetts, were all lined up near the eastern edge of the old North American continent. Hanover, New Hampshire, and Brattleboro, Vermont, were in a sliver of country with an average width of scarcely twenty miles that Zen called the Brompton-Cameron Terrane. He said it was not exotic. It seemed to be "a distal part of North America that was pushed onto the continent like a floe in an ice-jam— rammed in." Keene, New Hampshire, Amherst and Spring- field, Massachusetts, and much of the Connecticut River lay in a swath about seventy miles wide that he thinks is truly exotic and is a southerly reach of the Central Maine Terrane. "It is from the other side of the ocean," Zen said. Its outer boundary runs through Fitchburg, Massachusetts, where it is welded to the country east of it by the Fitchburg Pluton, a granite batholith. The country east of it was the Massabesic-Merrimack Terrane (Portsmouth and Nashua and Manchester, New Hampshire; Sturbridge, Massachu- setts; Storrs, Connecticut), which also came over the Iapetus Ocean. East of that—and including New London, Con- necticut, and Worcester, Massachusetts—was a bent, irreg- ular piece of the world as little as two and as much as seventy miles wide, of which Zen remarked, "God knows where it came from. It's a big enigma. It has no fossil control. It could be delaminated basement of the Massabesic- Merrimack Terrane. It is known as Nashoba." And, finally, through Cape Ann, Salem, Lynn, and Boston, nearly as far west as Worcester, and including Newport, Providence, and Plymouth, was New England's "most distinctly and un- equivocally exotic terrane," Atlantica.

Atlantica. Seaward of all the voyaging pieces that had collided in sequence, making mountains, Atlantica differed from the others in a clear and puzzling manner: it was not pervasively deformed. You don't crash head on into a con- tinent and take the shock of the tectonics undeformed. The successive collisions that preceded the arrival of Atlantica, which are collectively known as the Acadian Orogeny, had folded, faulted, and profoundly metamorphosed all the other terranes. In Atlantica, by contrast, even the gas cavities in Precambrian volcanic rocks are undeformed. Tiny shards are recognizable in Precambrian ash. In Atlantica, Zen said, Ordovician plutonic rocks are as fresh as the plutonic rocks of the Sierra Nevada, which are four hundred million years younger. In Atlantica, Silurian-Devonian volcanic and sedimentary rocks are undeformed. "In Acadian time, they were not touched."

"So where was Atlantica during the Acadian events?" I asked him.

He said, "I wish I knew. It's entirely conceivable that at the end of Acadian time you could have walked dry-shod from the Adirondacks to Atlantica—to Boston, but not where Boston is now. It would have been some hundreds of kilometres away; my prejudice would be to the south— a prejudice based on paleomagnetic data."

When the Acadian events were over and the mountains stood high, Atlantica, to remain undeformed, must have come sliding in along a transform fault, like southwestern New Zealand along the Alpine Fault, like southwestern California along the San Andreas Fault. Thus arrived Atlantica, from whose bedrock the ice sheet almost surely plucked up what became Plymouth Rock, and where, in any case, the Mayflower landed.

I said, "If you had to make a choice, where would you say Atlantica came from?"

He said, "Africa."

The rock reassembled is not a perfect fit, because so much of it is missing. On the seaward side, the walls of the great crack diverge concavely, like a clamshell. Cleaning out the old mortar, Choquette opened a space deep enough to hide a football. When he worked far inside, his entire forearm was in the rock. Also, he removed rotten mortar from the top of the buried portion—the cushioning mattress beneath the two joined segments that are visible to the visiting public. Sparks jumped from the cutting edge of his chisel. The visiting public, now two and three deep around the railings above, had come to Plymouth to see a cold, silent stone and were watching the trajectories of sparks. A man in a bright-red jacket with an American flag on one shoulder snapped the rock with a Japanese camera and said to his wife, "They're looking for fossils."

Plymouth is a red-brick-and-white-clapboard town that has cheerfully shouldered the burdens of its negotiable antiquity. Outside one store, the words "KARATE CHECHI" appear on an eighteenth-century oval wooden sign. Ye Olde Town Crier is some doors away from Hair Illusions. There are houses that were known to the original people (1640, 1666). The streets are neat, the park is attractive under Coles Hill beside the bay, where the rock in the cage reposes. The Mayflower in replica—a hundred and six feet long, a hundred and eighty-one tons, with a very high and narrow stern—floats at a pier nearby: a gift from the City of Plymouth in Devon. Plymouth, Massachusetts, averages something like three thousand visitors a day—ten thousand on Thanksgiving, and scarcely a slack moment in any part of the year. Ruth Walker, a retired science teacher who works for the state as an interpreter of the rock, once told me some of the questions that visitors frequently ask:

"How did he get all those animals on that boat?"

"Where are the Niña and the Pinta?"

"Why doesn't the rock say '1492'?"

"Where is the sword?"

A man once appeared with a boxer on a leash and asked if it would be all right if the dog "marked the rock."

A descendant will blush modestly, rub one Reebok against another, and announce that his name is Howland. With a glance over a shoulder at the hill above the rock, another man says his name is Coles. His billowing sports shirt cannot drape the fact that since 1620 he has eaten very well. A Soule says hello, he's related to George. Descendants seem to appear by the shipload. In their sneakers, their cowboy boots, their leather jackets and one-way shades, they are Fullers, Winslows, Whites, Brewsters, Billingtons, Warrens, Browns, Aldens, and mixed collaterals. Someone tells the story that as Massasoit watched the ship arrive he said, "There goes the neighborhood."

A great many people are disillusioned when they see the size of the rock. At some level of consciousness they have confused it with Gibraltar. If they are asked what they expected, a high percentage of them will actually mention Gibraltar. The extent of the letdown is this: Gibraltar is thirty million times as large as Plymouth's potatolike boulder. Visitors have called it "the biggest disappointment in New England." When Jim Jenkins, of Greensboro, North Carolina, saw it, he said, "I've turned over bigger rocks than this mowing grass."

Don Matinzi, who grew up in Plymouth, said, "I get very defensive about the rock. People ask, 'What did the Pilgrims do, fall over it?' They say, 'It's a pebble.' And so forth. I'd like to have some of these people experience the privation the Pilgrims did. Instead, they ask, 'Where's the sword?' " Matinzi—young, with rimless glasses and brown shoulder-length hair—is an artist, a photographer, and a graduate of the Art Institute in Boston, and helps to support himself as the park supervisor, watching over the rock.

When I asked him one day if he knew of many other erratics bestrewn through the Plymouth woods, he thought for a while and counted few. The great Laurentide Ice Sheet had not, in this region, been generous with large boulders. There was one on Sandwich Road called Sacrifice Rock. It was sacred to the Wampanoags, of whom Massasoit was chief. Even today, offerings will appear from time to time on Sacrifice Rock—handfuls of pebbles, branches of trees. Its actual name is Manitou Asseinah (God's Rock). It sits by the roadside unfenced. When we went to see it, Matinzi said, with some ambiguity, "This is the only rock that does have a history that relates to the area." The boulder had come to rest six and a half miles from Plymouth Rock. Coarse-grained, with large crystals of pink feldspar, it may have derived from greater depth.

Now in Plymouth, as a rising tide was threatening the efforts of Choquette, Matinzi was saying that an amazingly large percentage of the rock's annual visitors were from other nations. Among all the categories of people who come to Plymouth, non-Americans are an even larger group than retired people, schoolchildren, or Mayflower descendants. The cage at the moment was full of children. By the school-busload, kids in great numbers had been coming and going all morning: BEDFORD CHARTER SERVICE, BIDDEFORD SCHOOL DEPT, BOSTON PUBLIC SCHOOLS. Matinzi said, too, that since his own schooldays, in Plymouth, he had seen the rock shrink. "It has shrunk six to ten inches from each end in my lifetime," he remarked. It was Matinzi who had noticed the disintegration of the old patchwork mortar and reported the need for repair.

As Choquette tapped with his chisel, his twelve-year-old, Jonathan, stood with a hand on one end of the rock. He said, "This thing here, Daddy, it's vibrating very much." With a hose, Choquette had from time to time been flushing out the chiselled bed of mortar from beneath the upper half. In his application interview, many weeks earlier, he had told the engineers that he thought the upper and lower halves made such an ill fit that with the rotten mortar gone at least three feet of the upper half would be cantilevered, and now he was proving himself right. He washed out so much mortar that eight inches of space separated a considerable area of the upper rock from the Tory basement. A couple of tons, including the celebrated vertical crack that Choquette was meant to repair, was projecting in air. Jonathan felt the rock rocking. It was obvious now that steel pins or steel staples must be holding the upper part together, for mortar alone could not retain so much suspended weight.

Lest the rock split and crash while the schoolchildren watched, Choquette supported it with riprap from the shore, and refused to continue until the state provided a couple of tons of three-quarter-inch bluestone to pack in as a new bed for the upper rock. The tide was stopping him anyway. Evading the rubber barricade, it came up through the sand. It just developed around his feet and was soon on its way to his knees. Matinzi said that the midday rise the day before had been the highest non-storm tide in years. Today's would be much the same. Choquette climbed out of the cage. By noon, the rock was almost underwater.

Anne, another merchant ship, arrived in Plymouth in 1623, with something like sixty passengers, one of whom was John Faunce. He remained in Plymouth and raised a family, including a son named Thomas, who was born in 1647. The Old Comers, or First Comers, as the Mayflower people were called, were still very much around, and the young Faunce could not have helped knowing them. Myles Standish died when Thomas Faunce was nine years old,

William Bradford when Faunce was ten, John Howland when Faunce was twenty-six, and John Alden when Faunce was forty. By then, Faunce was keeper of the Plymouth Records. a job he performed for thirty-eight years. He also became the ruling elder of Plymouth's First Church. His mother's brother, Nathaniel Morton, was the colony historian. Thomas Faunce was what geologists call autochthonous; that is, he originated in Plymouth and he never moved. He was literally immobile—enfeebled, ninety-four years old—when the day came that the facts of his life assembled here acquired their collective relevance. Someone told Faunce that the big boulder on the harbor shore would soon be buried.

Faunce had himself driven downtown and carried the final distance sitting in a chair. The chair was set beside the boulder. In 1741, this was enough to attract a crowd. Like the countless thousands of historic objects that would be lost forever in coming years, the rock was scheduled to disappear in the foundations of a wharf. Faunce was there to prevent that. He told his listeners not to forget that this was the landing rock of the Old Comers. They would do well to show it appropriate respect.

Faunce had grown up on this story. And history selected him as the earliest person to mention it. In a hundred and twenty-one years, the boulder's role in the American narrative had in no surviving way been reported to the future. The first-rate and firsthand accounts in "Mourt's Relation" (1622) overlooked it. In a hundred and fifty thousand words William Bradford does not mention it—a fact that would carry more weight if Bradford had mentioned the Mayflower.

A couple of centuries of reverence rest on the hearsay of Thomas Faunce. People who believe in the rock say there is no obvious reason that any of his predecessors *would* mention it. And, besides, it was a Bradford characteristic to be aloof from details. More than twenty times its present size, the boulder was near the edge of the channel; the settlers may have connected it to the shore with planks and used it often. Believers align what few facts they can in a generally positive direction. Skeptics do the reverse. The middle ground does not seem crowded.

The late Samuel Eliot Morison, of Harvard, once Harmsworth Professor of American History at Oxford, and the editor of Bradford's journal (Knopf, 1952), received a letter in 1953 from Rose Briggs, a Plymouth regional historian, asking his help with a monograph she was preparing on the story of the rock. What to say about "the Elder Faunce tradition"? she wrote. "He could have known; he may have been senile. Clearly the town believed him."

By return mail came a note from Morison, written in a hand sufficiently illegible to have qualified him as a physician:

I see no reason to go back on Elder Faunce now. *The American Neptune* chart of P. Hbr 1780 . . . shows a 1-fm. channel coming up to the shore there. The Rock, at ½ tide could have been a convenient place from which to lay logs or hewn planks to high water mark for a dry landing of people and goods—very important in "that could countrie."

I do hope however that you will point out that the Rock as a landing applies only to Mayflower arriving . . . *not* to the Exploring Expedition. . . .

In an address I shall give to naval officers in Jan. I am going to compare the (hypothetical) logs or planks laid from Rock to shore. to the pontoon causeways we had to use on shelving landing beaches in World War II to land vehicles from LSTs.

Sincerely yours,
SEMorison

[211]

By two in the afternoon, the tide was in retreat, but the water was slow to leave the cage. It ponded there, higher than the surface of the harbor. Mark Cullinan, in hip waders, went down into the cage to bail out the rock. Paul Choquette, in twelve-inch yellow boots, joined him with another bucket. As they moved about, long microphone booms followed them, sparring over their heads. They were entertaining not only children now but ABC, NBC, CNN, and CBS. One mike was kept in a fixed position close to the top of the rock, not to miss a syllable if the rock had something to say.

When Choquette was able to resume work, he threw coffee into the small cavern he had opened, and watched it drip down the sides. Where mortar remained, the coffee turned the lime green. Choquette went after it with his chisel. Like a dentist doing his best with a split and cavitied tooth, he worked primarily on the inside, where he needed to prepare a clean, dry surface completely free of the old mortar. Jonathan held a flashlight for him, and together they created an odd tableau: a twelve-year-old boy shining a flashlight into the innards of Plymouth Rock while his father knelt beside him with both arms inserted to the elbows.

During this effort far within, the chisel removed a couple of flakes of the rock itself—fractions of an ounce. I asked for the flakes and Cullinan gave them to me. I wanted to take them to geologists at Princeton University and the United States Geological Survey to see what might be learned about the nature and origin of the boulder. In this era, a piece of rock of remarkably small size will serve the purposes of chemical and mineralogical analysis. In 1969, moon rocks as small as pinheads were sent to selected petrologists.

In Princeton, I took a flake to Douglas Johnson, the

departmental lapidarian, who removed some crystals and also sawed off a piece of the rock a thousandth of an inch thick. This so-called thin section, mounted on a glass slide and readied for a microscope, was added to a collection of thin sections that Johnson had made from rocks I had gathered in various localities north of Plymouth—Cape Ann, for example, the region of Cohasset, and Kingston, on the edge of Plymouth Bay. Romantically, I hoped for a matchup in the thin sections—for a strong indication of a place or places where the ice sheet could have ripped out the bedrock that it carried to Plymouth, fashioning en route the national boulder.

I sent the entire kit—all the thin sections and a smidgen of Plymouth Rock—to E-an Zen, in Reston. The rock travelled Federal Express. In the morning, Zen looked at it with a hand lens and a microscope, called me on the telephone, and told me what he saw. First of all, Plymouth Rock was granite. It appeared to be Dedham granite, a major component of the Atlantica Terrane. "I'm convinced that it is a piece of the Dedham," he said. "Where the rock is freshest, the feldspar is distinctly pink, which is characteristic of the Dedham. The thin section shows a wedge-shaped crystal that is brownish blood red. That is a crystal of sphene. The blood-red sphene is distinctive of the Dedham. There are two distinct original feldspars. The potassium feldspar is in a form called perthite, and the plagioclase feldspar has become a highly altered saussurite, rimmed by an inclusion-free zone of sodium-rich plagioclase, all of which is also characteristic of the Dedham."

For reasons unfathomable, I had hoped that one of my numerous samples from the plutons of Cape Ann would match up with Plymouth Rock, like two setts of the same tartan. If so, the boulder could be said to have derived from the bedrock of Gloucester and traversed what is now Massachusetts Bay to come to rest in Plymouth. In Zen's lineup, however, all those samples were clear losers. "The Cape Ann granite contains only one feldspar," he said. "Like the Peabody granite and, for that matter, the Quincy granite. Moreover, they are gray granites. You never see pinkish feldspar in the surface of those granites. Plymouth Rock is not one of them."

He said, incidentally, that the quartz in Plymouth Rock had been "deformed very thoroughly."

I recalled his telling me that the Atlantica Terrane was undeformed.

"Atlantica is shot through with local faults," he said. "Plymouth Rock could have sheared along a fault zone. In almost any outcrop of the Dedham, you can see that. Plymouth Rock is a piece of the Dedham that has deformed in the solid state. This is not a pervasive deformation. It's a local fault, a crushing of the rock rather than a plastic deformation. If you go to Minute Man National Historical Park, where the Battle of Lexington was fought, you see Dedham granite that was very much sheared up in the Bloody Bluff Fault Zone. Plymouth Rock is locally sheared more than usual. Almost surely, when the boulder cracked it broke naturally along a weak zone formed by the shears. That is what the mason was repairing."

Looking further into the Plymouth thin section, he discerned that the biotite in the original granite had been recrystallized in the fault zone, becoming sugary and smoky green. There was also a lot of epidote. He said, "Epidote, saussuritized plagioclase, potassic feldspar, and the presence of sphene are distinctive of late Precambrian granitic rocks in the Boston area, of which the Dedham is an example."

So where did E-an Zen think Plymouth Rock derived from?

He said, "Somewhere between Boston and Plymouth Bay, I would guess. The ice direction was south-southeast. So the rock would have come north by northwest."

Within any large body of granite, there are countless minor variations. Compared with Plymouth Rock, the samples I had taken south of Boston from the Cohasset region through Weymouth to Kingston were close in nature but not identical.

I said, "How far northwest?"

"You cannot go beyond Concord and Lexington, because there you leave Atlantica," he said. "There is no rock like this except in Atlantica. It's a very, very distinctive rock."

PLYMOUTH ROCK AFRICAN

The Dedham granite, Zen added, had been radiometrically dated at six hundred and eight million years. That was when, in some far-distant land, the cooling magma froze as rock—a date that could be looked upon as accurate within seventeen million years.

In Plymouth, that week before Thanksgiving, darkness came early and quickly, and it left the television crews with nothing to see. They departed, but the visiting public kept arriving, even after dusk. They had not come to be on television or to witness the master Choquette. They knew nothing about the repair. They were drawn, like everyone else in all seasons, by the stone that is treasured by a great nation, its very dust shared as a relic. They were surprised, all of them, to find so much activity in a place that ordinarily has the aspect of a tomb. I remember particularly a young man from Florida and his companion, a woman from California, who clambered down the riprap to the harbor shore, the better to peer into the cage. The sound of the chisel was as rhythmic as a drum. The flashlight brightened in the growing darkness. The young man from Florida had shoulder-length gray hair. His friend was a waist-length-waterfall blonde and wore a black leather coat that nearly reached her shoes. He was wearing a Christmas-red sweatshirt decorated with large script that said "Dear Santa, I want it all." Apparently, it all was in Plymouth. He was exuberant. "What luck! What luck!" he kept saying. "What luck to find all this going on! My girlfriend wanted to stop here. I didn't. We argued in the car. She insisted that we come. And I said to her, 'It's a rock! Nothing ever happens to it.' "